MEASURING
what MATTERS

D1466648

MEASURING
what MATTERS

**Accountability and the
Great Commission**

BY DAVE STRAVERS

Mission India
PO Box 141312
Grand Rapids, Michigan 49514-1312
877.644.6342
www.missionindia.org

MEASURING WHAT MATTERS: *Accountability and the Great Commission*
© 2012 David Stravers
Published by Mission India, Grand Rapids, Michigan

ISBN: 978-0-9788551-6-1

First printing, 2012.

Printed in the United States of America.

1 2 3 4 5 Printing / Year 15 14 13 12

Design by Julie Folkert

TABLE OF CONTENTS

Introduction

"What's on the mind of America?" That was the assignment for a group of graduate students sent by their Professor of Sociology at a Midwestern university to shopping malls in two large cities. They were to interview shoppers at random in order to discover what people are most concerned about.

What they discovered confirms an observation being made by many students of 21st century American society: Americans are searching for significance. Those sociology students distilled the American search for significance into three questions that 21st century shoppers are asking:

Why should I get out of bed in the morning?
How can I make it through another stressful day?
Will anything I do today really make a difference?

Christian believers can identify with these comments. We spend most of our adult lives striving for significance. The longer we live, the more pressing this issue becomes for us. When we start approaching the end of our lives, will we be able to look back and say, "Look—I made a difference"?

The search for significance can lead to good things, or it can chase after evil. Even terrorists are searching for significance when they blow themselves up in the twisted hope of transforming their own deaths into something of lasting value. For others, the search for significance becomes a consuming materialism—an insatiable desire to accumulate wealth. The clichéd bumper sticker is no less the life's pursuit of today's culture: "Whoever dies with the most toys, wins!"

Some search for significance by way of fame or respect. Others search for significance by positively pouring their energies into children and grand-children, providing for their education and material security. We want our accomplishments to outlast us.

For a follower of Jesus, the ultimate significance lies in those things that cannot pass away, that can never disappoint, and that will survive not only death, but also the fiery cleansing of God's judgment. We followers of Jesus know the search for significance inevitably will focus on the coming of the Kingdom of God. We identify with the Apostle Paul, who discovered his eternal significance in the call to prepare the world for Christ's return. A spiritual war is raging, Christ's followers are His agents in that war, and He invites us to contribute to His ultimate victory.

For us, the hunger for significance becomes a matter of how we can best contribute to the victory of Christ. The *Missio Dei*, Mission of God, one of the unifying themes of the Scriptures, defines the scope and objectives of Christ's victory. As most succinctly summarized in Jesus' last words on earth recorded in the four Gospels and the Book of Acts, the Mission of God compels me to make disciples, to present the Gospel to those who have not yet heard, and to be Christ's witness in the whole world as a testimony to all people everywhere.

But how can I know whether and to what extent I am contributing in a significant way to His Great Commission? That question is the central topic of this publication: how do we measure significance in terms of the Kingdom of God? How do we keep score according to God's priorities?

{ 1

The Mission Versus the Missionaries

As a boy attending church in Battle Creek, Michigan, I heard the stories of furloughed missionaries who told of trekking great distances to remote villages in "the bush" of Northern Nigeria. The long trip by ocean liner from USA to Africa meant that furloughs were few and far between. I read the biography of James Hudson Taylor who in a much earlier era took an even longer ocean voyage from England to China. He walked from one Chinese city to the other, attracting crowds of thousands (and often physical beatings) simply because he was the first white man they had ever seen. Such stories ignited my adventurous spirit. Many years later, when my wife Jan and I boarded a plane for Taipei, Taiwan, the trans-Pacific trip lasted only a few hours (making it much easier to return home for a visit after only 12 months on the field). Our mission field was already heavily populated by missionaries, American military personnel, Western businessmen, and most significant of all, by hundreds of thousands of home-grown Chinese believers worshiping in thousands of congregations.

My first meeting with the larger missionary team in

Taiwan was a full-scale immersion into the most pressing issue of the modern missions movement: Western versus indigenous outreach. One missionary was studying Taiwanese because he wanted to do grass roots church planting among Taiwanese speaking people. Another missionary argued passionately that this was a waste of time and resources, because there were already thousands of native Taiwanese-speaking believers who could do this better than any foreigner. The real need, he argued, was for training and material support to empower local believers. The home office was non-committal about this burning issue—their greater concern seemed to be for putting as many missionary boots on the field as possible, regardless.

As the newest member of the team, I was assigned to do evangelism while teaching English to university students. I felt ambivalent at the time about this debate. But the objectivity of time and distance leaves no doubt in my mind which was the right perspective: empowering the national believer to bring the Gospel into his or her own community.

Making Disciples of All Nations

There was a time when it seemed that the only way to fulfill Christ's Great Commission (Matthew 28:19) was to send missionaries to far-away places. Entire geo-political nations were devoid of Christian witness. Those who did not know Jesus were so far removed from those who did know Him that the only way to reach the lost was for some people to travel long distances, learn new languages, and take up residence in new and strange communities.

Cross cultural missionaries traveled across oceans, risked their lives, and many never returned. Those who were able to return home to their "sending churches" recounted stories of both success and failure. Supporters back home rejoiced at the heroism of missionaries like William Carey, David Livingstone, Adoniram Judson, and James Hudson Taylor. Thousands were inspired to imitate them.

Christian believers in the "sending countries" began to assume that the only way to obey the Great Commission was to become a missionary and travel to a far away place. The Great Commission became the "Great *Commissionary*," as if Jesus had commanded, "Send missionaries to all nations."

The "mission versus missionary" issue can be seen in many other situations. I've had the privilege, for instance, of having three different medical doctors as close long-time personal friends. Their lives diverged into radically different directions. Dr. Don has practiced for more than 30 years in the same location, same specialization, and even lived in the same house for all that time. Medicine for him has been simply an occupation that enables him to live comfortably and pursue his preferred lifestyle. Dr. Al, on the other hand, became disillusioned with traditional medicine, jumped into one related field after another, and the last time we talked he still expressed significant frustration and dissatisfaction with his life and work.

My third friend, Dr. Russell Atonson, was born in the Philippines and trained in the US. He has given his whole life to serving the poorest of the poor in developing countries. He has a mission in life that has transformed his medical degree into marching orders for the Kingdom of God. The fact that he is a medical doctor is secondary to achieving his mission, and the means by which he seeks to fulfill the calling God has given him.

During my first trip to mainland China, the first person I met was Dr. Wang, a young person who had just recently come to know the Lord Jesus Christ. Wang was a medical intern working in Guangzhou, China. He was struggling with how to apply his new-found faith to practicing medicine in a highly restricted authoritarian environment. Even our casual conversation had to be conducted in a private setting, to avoid endangering him. Wang and I did not discuss my three doctor-friends, but if he had asked me to recommend models that he might emulate, there is no question which of my three friends I would have recommended to him.

The "Real" Missionary

The world has changed. Starting about 40 years ago, Western Christians began to take seriously this fact. Many Great Commission Christians began to realize that two centuries of Great Commission activity had successfully implanted the Gospel in almost every geo-political nation.

Even ethnic groups that were entirely devoid of Christian witness were living within striking distance of Christian communities who did not have to travel across oceans to reach them.

In many cases, nearby Christians did not need to learn another language in order to reach the lost, because they already spoke the language and shared a similar culture with the unreached. Even when nearby believers needed to learn a new language to reach a different ethnic group, they could often do so more effectively than a Westerner, and at far less expense. Some proclaimed a "revolution in world missions."

A new paradigm was born—one that encouraged Western Christians to send or support "native missionaries" as opposed to Western missionaries. Organizations such as Partners International, Christian Aid Mission, Gospel for Asia, E3 Partners, Advancing Native Missions, Bible League, and Mission India have in various ways advocated that supporting gifted national workers is the best expression of our responsible stewardship of Great Commission resources.

Some mission leaders have argued against this new paradigm, claiming that the only true missionary is the cross-cultural worker, not the native worker; or claiming that native workers are not necessarily more effective than their expatriate counterparts. They want to argue that "real" missionaries are those who "cross cultural barriers with the Gospel," and we should reserve the label *missionary* for those who cross significant barriers. They also claim that a church that stops sending her sons and daughters to far away mission fields will also stop caring about the Great Commission.

However one defines *missionary*, the fact is that sending disciple-makers in the sense of the Great Commission is an activity that is now directed, encouraged, and funded by churches on all continents, especially by those that until recently were considered to be "missionary receiving" countries. Ironically, in fact, the most rapid growth in sending missionaries has come in those places that used to be considered "missionary receiving" countries.

Counting the Costs

Perhaps the most persuasive and frequent argument for the new paradigm of supporting native workers is that non-Western workers typically cost only a fraction as much to support as Westerners. The cost to send a Western Christian to live and work in a foreign country averages more than $75,000 per year, and in many cases the cost is much higher. Cost is a major obstacle for many prospective missionaries who feel that they have heard God's Great Commission call.

Christian workers sent from a non-Western country can often work for a fraction of this cost. In India, for instance, it is argued that a well-trained Indian national pastor can "do the work of a foreign missionary" for less than $1,500 per year. For the cost of one Westerner, someone could support a team of 50 native missionaries.

Even more compelling, these 50 missionaries either would not need to learn a new language, or they would learn the new language much more quickly and more effectively than their Western counterpart would be able to, resulting in further cost savings.

The Western Church in particular must come to terms with the revolutionary change in demographics that has rocked the worldwide Christian church in the past 40 years. In 1960, approximately two-thirds of all Christians worldwide lived in Western countries. Today, believers in the poor countries of the non-Western world, in what is being called the "Global South," far outnumber those in the wealthy West. What they need most is not Western bodies, but Western resources. Believers in the West, despite being outnumbered two-to-one, still control 85% of all Christian resources, and therefore are in the best position to channel God's material and financial blessings to His front-line national workers.

My wife and I had been living and working as missionaries in Bacolod City, Philippines for two years when we established a Bible College and received our first incoming students, almost all teenagers. Among them was Nestor, who had been a Christian believer for only three months. Nestor was only 16 years old and knew very little about the Bible. He knew that Jesus had died and risen, but understood few of the basics of the Christian faith.

His second weekend as a freshman student, Nestor and his classmates were assigned to go out for "field work" responsibilities, leading evangelistic Bible studies and doing door-to-door witnessing. Nestor was sent to a city several hours away where he had relatives. We gave him 12 copies of a little Bible course called "*Sino ang Dios?*" (Who is God?). I wondered how he would do.

The day after the students returned from their weekend, I opened the class time by asking for volunteers to report on how their weekend went. Nestor eagerly raised his hand. His report went something like this:

"It was very exciting. All day Saturday I walked around inviting people to come to my Bible study. On Sunday night, 14 people showed up at my auntie's house. We studied the Bible for two hours. At the end, four people said that they wanted to receive Jesus and prayed with us the sinner's prayer. Everyone asked me to come back next weekend to lead another class."

The teacher asked, "Nestor, what did you teach them during those two hours?"

Nestor simply beamed, "Well—everything I know! . . . I don't know what I am going to teach them next week."

Nestor kept going back. Others went to help him. Today there is a Christian church in that neighborhood.

During my last year serving as a missionary in the Philippines, my family and I were paid a salary of about $20,000. By this time, we had been speaking Hiligaynon for ten years, and my wife and I were doing our best to teach classes in a Bible College, witness to the people in our area, and start a new church. I have to admit, however, that my effectiveness as a Gospel communicator was far inferior to the skills of the teenage students in the Bible College where I taught. Even my students who were new Christians were more effective disciple-makers than I was. They won scores of converts and started new churches at a pace that I could not begin to match. If it took me five years to plant a new church, they could plant two or three churches in that time.

These students were being supported at a cost of less than $500 per year, and the highest salary being paid to a Filipino pastor in my area was about $2,000. Do the math: for the cost to support me as a missionary, you could have employed a team of 40 Filipino believers with results one hundred times greater than mine!

These comparisons should not surprise us. The first missionary teams, Paul and Barnabas, and later Paul and Silas, consisted mainly of bi-cultural workers who were already able to speak the language of their target audiences. They did not need to study their target culture and language for years on end.

However, in the one case where they encountered a strange foreign tongue, they had great difficulty in explaining the Gospel message. In fact, Paul himself was eventually stoned by a mob and presumed dead (Acts 14:8-20).

{ 2

More Effective Workers

A few years after the opening of the former Soviet Union, a large group of Russian pastors was meeting together for fellowship and prayer in Almaty, Kazakhstan. During the time for prayer requests, one pastor suggested, "Let's pray that China will become open to the Gospel, just as happened in our own country." Another pastor chimed in, "Yes, perhaps then the American missionaries will leave here and all go to China!"

The natural hostility in many developing countries to Western influence on local customs can be a significant hindrance to the Gospel message. This is another crucial reason why national missionaries can be the better means to overseas disciple making. A more compelling reason than cost is the reality of the national workers usually being more effective than their Western counterparts. They often already understand the culture of the people they are serving, can learn to speak their language more fluently, and will not be viewed with the same suspicion as a white-faced foreigner.

In most developing countries today, people much prefer their own cultural ways and are hostile to or suspicious of Western practices. There is no doubt that the rapid growth of the Gospel in China during the 1970s and 1980s was partly due to the policy of the Chinese government starting in the 1950s to expel all Westerners, nationalize all Western religious institutions, close down all Western-looking churches, and forbid all contact between Chinese and Western believers. As a result, the church in China was purged of foreign influence and severed from foreign connections. The Chinese government unwittingly removed the greatest single obstacle to the Gospel during the previous 150 years of mission work. As a result, the church exploded in both numbers of believers and in spiritual commitment to Christ. The resulting conversion of a hundred million Chinese people far surpassed in numbers anything that has happened in the previous 2,000 years of church history.

A similar event started in India in the 1960s when the government stopped granting missionary visas. Can it be mere coincidence that, 40 years later, India is now open to the Gospel as never before in history; or mere coincidence that the fastest growing churches in India have no denominational affiliations with foreigners? Church leaders in India now pray expectantly that millions of their country-men will turn to Christ, with every reason to believe that within this generation a church will be established in every Indian community.

Connecting the Skills

It would be wrong to conclude that there should be no more Western missionaries sent anywhere. Western workers sometimes have skills that are still lacking in non-Western settings: for instance in Bible translation, counseling, and seminary teaching. However, the relevant skills that Westerners can bring often do not include evangelism and discipleship. Indigenous workers almost always are far more effective in achieving Great Commission objectives.

I first became acutely aware of my comparative ineffectiveness as a missionary in the Philippines, sent to train Filipino evangelists who could already do the job better than I could. After leaving the Philippines, I traveled in many different countries, and the lesson kept repeating itself, perhaps never more dramatically than during my first visit to India.

I was participating in an all-day worship celebration with about 200 new believers from the Yanadi tribe living in the southern state of Andhra Pradesh. Midway through the afternoon activities, Pastor Kamalakar, the Indian worship leader, paused our services and said, "Now it's time for healing the sick. Let's divide into small groups, and a pastor will lead each group to heal those around you." Kamalakar came over to me, took my arm, and led me to a woman I had previously noticed who had been rolling around on the ground, apparently in agony, all during our day-long activities. He said, "Pastor Stravers, this woman has a demon. You cast out this demon. While you are doing that, I need to go over there to pray for another person."

I felt like telling him, "You don't understand. I have two theology degrees, but I did not learn how to do this in seminary." He left me no choice. Fortunately, there were several other believers sitting on the ground nearby, all of them Indian women. So I recruited them, we surrounded the demonized woman, laid our hands on her, and all prayed out loud together. I prayed in English, while they prayed in Telugu and Yanadi, and perhaps some other languages that I did not recognize.

After a few minutes of praying and nothing happened, I did not know what to do. I remembered what Jesus did, so I looked at the woman and said, "Demon, if you are in there, we command you to leave this woman." I later realized that if the other believers had spoken English, they probably would have thought, "Why did this pastor say, 'Demon, *if* you are in there'? Doesn't he see that she has a demon? What's wrong with him?"

We prayed some more. Nothing happened. Kamalakar reconvened our meeting and called us to order. The woman sat up, rubbed her eyes as if she had been sleeping. No one paid much attention to her. By the end of the service, she was standing and talking with her family and friends. Kamalakar came over to me. "Praise the Lord!" he said, "This woman has been delivered! The demon is gone!"

"It is?" I said. "Are you sure? Perhaps it will return?"

Kamalakar looked at me with great shock. "Don't say such a thing! Of course the demon is gone. It will not return! God has delivered her!"

I remained skeptical. Two weeks later I received a letter from Kamalakar stating that the woman had been reunited with her family and was worshipping with the other believers. He even wrote to my boss thanking him for sending me to India, saying, "The demons fled at his command." This was very polite of him to say, but I knew better. It was the spiritual insight and faith of the Indians that carried the day. I was only a spectator. God and the Indian believers were teaching me about demons and faith.

The realization that native Christians who already live in non-Western countries can do the Great Commission better continues to grow among Western churches and mission agencies. More and more believers in the West have accepted the challenge to support national workers who don't need to cross the ocean or live the Western lifestyle. They usually know far more about prayer and spiritual warfare than Westerners. National workers now travel to the USA seeking additional support for their ministries. Many American believers gladly help them, believing that they can represent Christ more effectively than a Western missionary.

Compassion Myopia

A challenge of the support-nationals paradigm is that the

focus can still remain on the wrong thing. After all, in Matthew 28:19 Jesus did not say, "Go and support national workers in all nations" or "Go and build worship buildings in all nations."

Yet our compassion has often been directed toward the existing church or the mission worker, all the while effectively ignoring the lost people who need Jesus. For good reason we may marvel when we hear the worker, whether American or Chinese, telling us about the hostile environment, the sufferings of his family, and the difficulties he faces. Our hearts should go out to the missionary, to the national worker, and to their families. But what should be our primary focus?

It was 1993 and I was sitting in a crowded hotel room in Beijing with twelve American tourists who were visiting China for the first time. Mr. and Mrs. Lin, a Chinese couple about 30 years old, were sharing their story with us. They were itinerant evangelists, wanted by the police, and had been fleeing from village to village while preaching the Gospel. They told us that everywhere they went, Chinese people were interested to hear about Jesus, and that they had personally baptized hundreds of new believers. They told us that a new church was started in every village that they visited. The Americans listened politely, and then it was time for questions:

An American Christian asked, "Mrs. Lin, how many children do you have?"

"Oh, we have no children," was her reply. "We have

decided that due to our lifestyle, we cannot have children. We have no permanent home, and so we have given up the possibility of children for the sake of the Gospel."

Another queried, "If you have no home, where do you keep your stuff?"

Mrs. Lin was perplexed: "What is 'stuff'?"

"You know . . . where is your furniture, your clothes, and your other possessions?"

Mrs. Lin pointed to a small suitcase. "All of our possessions are in that bag."

There was stunned silence in the room. Two of the Americans started weeping. The American visitors did not know what else to say, until one man said, "Please, can we pray for you now?" The Americans were blown away by the commitment of these two workers.

The exchange itself is compelling, and we have good cause to contrast our priorities. But it was the personal stories of these two workers that had touched hearts in a way that the conversions of thousands had not. It's not that the Americans did not care about the reports of so many Chinese people who had been given eternal life; rather, it is indicative of how we focus and prioritize our passions and compassion.

The experience of a missionary couple in Venezuela similarly illustrates the difference between compassion for the worker and compassion for the lost. The couple had moved to Caracas, a modern but thoroughly pagan city. Their early letters to supporters told about their high-rise apartment residence, and the great need for the Gospel in this huge city. After only a few months, their sending agency reported that gifts were not coming in for their support as expected. There was a question whether they could continue the work.

Then, without thinking much about it, the missionaries mentioned in their monthly prayer letter that when they got up in the morning and turned on the faucet in the kitchen sink, cockroaches came swarming out of the drain. They mentioned this daily event in passing, a single sentence buried in their two-page letter. A few weeks later, their sending agency sent them amazing news: donations had come pouring in for their support. Their American partners suddenly realized that, even though the missionaries lived in a modern city, they were "real" missionaries who were "really suffering" for the sake of the Gospel. It's hard to escape the implications that their support was largely based not on compassion for the lost souls in Caracas, but on compassion for the missionaries who had to deal with cockroaches in their kitchen sink.

It's not necessarily so different for those who support national workers. A pastor from India was invited to speak in an all-white suburban church service. His facial complexion, accented English, and contagious enthusiasm endeared him immediately to the congregation. He showed photos of his wife and children. When he told stories about the sub-standard living conditions of the pastors in India, and stories about physical attacks from

Hindu extremists, the people had compassion on him. Many asked, "What can we do to help you?"

Obviously it's not that we are wrong to be motivated by compassion for the suffering missionary or national worker. Compassion has its place in the Great Commission strategies that are needed to bring about the Great Completion pictured for us in Revelation. In fact, in Matthew 25:31-46, our Lord demands compassion for His suffering brothers.

However, we do need to be willing to measure our motives and purpose by more than emotion. Being good stewards means clearly defining our spiritual objectives and honestly evaluating how best to use our resources to achieve those objectives. Dale Galvin aptly sums up this same challenge for non-profits today: "Finding the right measure is the holy grail of proving the worth of a nonprofit. However, focusing on the wrong measure . . . can have very undesirable effects."* Honestly weighing our purposes and priorities should move us beyond gut reactions—beyond how deeply we care about the suffering of the workers. It takes some purposeful shifting of our vision and motives toward a care that is also for the salvation of the lost.

---

* Dale Galvin, "Tiny Bubbles: A Guide to the New Nonprofit Economy," *The Nonprofit Quarterly*, Summer 2006, p. 33.

{ 3

Staying Focused by Measuring What Matters

Jesus certainly cares about the suffering of His disciples, especially those disciples who have committed their lives to His Commission. When the Scriptures describe Jesus' compassion, however, a significant focus is upon the lost. "He had compassion on them because they were harassed and helpless, like sheep without a shepherd" (Matthew 9:36). Jesus' compassion for the lost sheep is why in the very next breath he urged his disciples, "Ask the Lord of the harvest, therefore, to send out workers into his harvest field" (Matthew 9:38).

It's the harvest field for which Jesus is especially concerned. It's the only reason to send out workers. We pray for Christ's workers not for their own sake, but because there is a great harvest waiting to be gathered. Today many of Christ's workers suffer because they are working in the spiritual harvest field, but they are seeking to bring others to know the Savior, just as in the Book of Acts.

As missionaries living under harsh conditions in the rural Philippines, my family deeply appreciated the concerns and prayers of our supporting churches back home. When my wife was laid low by illness, when my son was injured by an accident, or when we all just tired of the endless stresses of our daily lives, we were encouraged so much by the loving concerns of supporters in America. However, we also knew that it simply was not good enough for our friends back home to keep us living in the Philippines.

We personally knew suffering missionaries and workers in the Philippines who were accomplishing little; and their supporters loved them too. But the Great Commission cannot be accomplished simply because a Christian worker is laboring somewhere under harsh conditions.

The Great Competition

Ask any avid fan of soccer, baseball, or American football what it is that gets them excited when the World Cup, World Series, or Super Bowl roll around. Is it enough that your home team fields the full complement of players? Is it enough that the required number of uniformed bodies are out on the field exercising their skills or receiving their lumps? If a professional golfer enters a tournament with the intention of just playing the holes but not bothering to keep score, how long will he or she last in the PGA? What is it that gets the stadium rocking with cheers, and what is it that appears in the headlines following the big game?

It's the score. It's what the players accomplish. The headlines don't scream "Home Team Fields Full

Complement of Players!" The headlines scream, "Home Team Wins 3-0!"

Sometimes people protest, *Let's not keep score. Let's play the game just for fun.* This means that one side or the other does not want to acknowledge the inherent competition in a game, or that they are just not willing to put forth the effort that competition demands.

Too often, the church has been satisfied just to field the players. We send out missionaries or national workers to do battle for the Great Commission, but we don't look at the score. We just ignore the fact that we are in the middle of a terrible knock-down, drag-out battle for the souls of human beings. We only seem to care that someone is in the game, rather than care whether we are winning or losing souls. Or are we playing at making disciples "just for fun," convinced there is no opposition and thus no competition, or simply unwilling to give it our best effort?

A Need for Harvesters

When Jesus sent out the seventy-two workers, He told them clearly why they were being sent: "The harvest is plentiful, but the workers are few. Ask the Lord of the harvest, therefore, to send out workers into his harvest field" (Luke 10:2). He did not say, "I have 72 willing workers. Therefore I will send them out to look for a harvest." The harvest was the reason, the focus, and the expected outcome of the sending. Because of the ripe harvest, the disciples are asked to pray for enough workers to bring it in. A worker who is not bringing in the harvest is therefore not completing the task for which he was sent. (See also Matt. 9:37-38.)

"By their fruit you will recognize them" (Matt. 7:20) applies to missionaries and Gospel workers as much as to anyone else. We can know who is doing the Great Commission work of Christ by the observable fruit of their ministry. Jesus clearly described the fruit of the Great Commission ministries that He most fervently desires when he said, "Make disciples of all nations" (Matt. 28:19).

Making disciples means bringing people out of darkness into the light. Making disciples means establishing new congregations of believers who worship together in places that never before had a Christian church. It's not enough to go. It's not enough to preach. It's not enough to be sent. The only means by which any ministry can be enough is when it is transformed by God's Holy Spirit and produces fruit.

The Triumph of God's Spirit

Making disciples means transforming people by the power of the Holy Spirit. Making disciples means baptizing people who have put their trust in Jesus. If he has been successful in his job, the missionary or native worker, when he dies or returns home, leaves behind the "disciple fruit" to continue to grow and prosper. If not, then the Great Commission has not been advanced.

This is the way God's Spirit works. "Disciple fruit"

can be seen. The stories of lives changed can be told and spiritual results can be counted. The Book of Acts is full of stories and also of numbers that describe the fruit of the Great Commission ministries of the disciples. To cite just a few:

- Three thousand people believed and were baptized (Acts 2:41).
- Five thousand men (not including women and children) believed (Acts 4:4).
- An Ethiopian official was baptized (Acts 8:38).
- A provincial governor named Sergius Paulus put his faith in Jesus (Acts 13:12).
- Four new churches were started: Iconium, Derbe, Lystra, and Pisidia (Acts 13:13-14:25).
- Prominent Greek men and many Greek women came to faith in Berea (Acts 17:12).
- Individuals were won to faith in Christ and churches were established in Philippi, Berea, Thessalonica, Athens, Corinth, and Ephesus (Acts 17-19).
- Many thousands of Jews believed (Acts 21:20).

The main work of the Holy Spirit in the Book of Acts was making disciples through the activities of Christ's followers. That work has not changed. Followers of Jesus are still making disciples among people who are hearing about Jesus for the first time. The accomplishment of this goal is still the primary measure of success. Our success is dependent on the work of the Holy Spirit, who sovereignly moves some to believe, and who often moves among entire nations so that millions are ready to hear and believe as never before. By focusing on those places where God is already at work, Great Commission Christians can witness miracles of conversion that surpass anything reported in the Book of Acts.

Are we prepared to celebrate the Holy Spirit's great victories? More people have come to Christ in the past 100 years than in the previous 1,900 years of church history.[*] And most of this growth came in the last 40 years. How many believers living today are aware of the continuing great openness to the Gospel among the largest population groups? For 1,900 years the great population centers like China, India, and Indonesia had yielded few converts. Many observers believe that the next forty years will totally eclipse what happened in the last forty, meaning that God's Spirit will likely accomplish even more astounding growth, and sooner rather than later.

Yet this imminent victory of the Gospel is not widely known, partly because our attentions have been diverted. We get immersed in godly enough activities; but they don't contribute to the results we say we care about. Rather than finding ways to connect ourselves to the

---

[*] "Status of Global Mission 2011," Center for the Study of Global Christianity, accessed January 27, 2011.
http://www.gordonconwell.edu/resources/documents/StatusOfGlobalMission.pdf

world's ripe harvest fields, we allow ourselves to stay stuck in unproductive fields (often in our own communities) where the soil yields rocks and weeds rather than spiritual fruit. It's telling that, rather than looking for victory stories of God's Spirit bringing people into the Kingdom, we are satisfied to dwell almost exclusively upon the trials and tribulations of the human workers.

{ 4

Great Commission Detours

My co-worker and I were visiting new churches in central Ghana on behalf of the Bible League and had just endured five hours in a crowded jeep bouncing down a pot-holed two-track. My knees, leg muscles, and stomach were aching from the jarring, tortuous trek through 100 degree heat. Finally we arrived, and as our jeep drove into the open area in the middle of the village, we saw 150 people seated in rows, facing a stage and awning that had been prepared for us, exuberantly singing a welcome song. How long they had been waiting, I have no idea.

Everyone watched as we were ushered to the chairs, sat down facing our audience, and politely accepted the formal greetings from the village elders. Their spokesman said, "I think you have had a long, hot journey. We have prepared some refreshment for you." A beautiful young woman then came up to us holding a large serving tray upon which were balanced two tall glasses of murky water.

My friend and I looked at each other. What do we do now? It was not merely a question of drinking muddy water. This part of Ghana was infested with dracunculiasis, or "Guinea worm"—a very painful parasitic disease that is contracted when a person drinks stagnant water contaminated with the larva of the Guinea worm. The larva develops in the bloodstream and eventually emerges from a skin blister as a long worm. Once a blister or open sore is submerged in water, the adult worm releases thousands of larvae, contaminating the water supply and leading to further infections—very unpleasant, to say the least.

Water contaminated by Guinea worm looks exactly like the water in those two glasses. The members of the audience were all intently watching us, presumably assuming that we would do the only polite action possible, and drink the contaminated water.

My friend and I hesitated. At this point, the Village Chief came to our rescue. Beaming a broad smile, he gestured to the two glasses and said, "As you can see, the only water supply for our entire village is contaminated by Guinea worm. We desperately need a well to be dug in our village, yet we don't have the means to dig one. We hope that you will help us."

The chief had made his point. We could hardly imagine the rate of infection and suffering among the residents of that village. And at that stage, it would have been very easy, even a relief, for us to pledge help to dig a well in that village. The chief was counting on this, and did very well to hide his disappointment when we did not respond by making that commitment.

The Bible League had decided, long before, to focus

exclusively on church planting and evangelism outcomes, not to become sidelined or diverted by the many other worthy needs that presented themselves to us. We were able to refer the villagers to other organizations that had been called to provide for such health needs.

The Discipline of Focus

If you are not measuring your progress, then it's easy to get sidelined, to get distracted by things that don't necessarily have a bearing on the final outcome. Detours happen when we send workers or send finances in a way that fails to produce the desired outcomes, or in the case of the Great Commission, the fruit of new disciples.

Many churches today have become distracted by focusing their missions primarily upon activities that are not very productive for the Great Commission. Our shrinking world has made international travel easier for everyone. Exotic destinations that once were reached only by missionaries or diplomats are now presented as vacation alternatives. Some Western Christians have even found a way to combine vacation urges with missionary efforts. The fastest growing missionary activity is the "short-term mission trip":

- Instead of sending a missionary to live, our focus is upon sending church members to visit.

- Instead of sending a missionary who has been trained to minister cross-culturally, we focus primarily upon sending our young people.

- Instead of learning the language, we only use English, hopefully with help from a translator.

- Instead of adapting to the culture, we just do it our own way, and hope against hope that the listener can figure it out without being offended.

- Instead of focusing on the spiritual, we focus on the physical.

- Instead of investing our finances in ministry that produces disciples, we invest in airline tickets and hotel rooms.

Some short-term mission trips work well for the Great Commission. Others do not. Consider the following parable of the short-term team that returned triumphant from their short-term mission trip.

A large congregation in Central California (for the sake of confidentiality let's call it "Grace Church") organized a short-term mission trip to Guatemala. Ten young people and eight adults spent ten days in a Guatemalan community. While three of the adults conducted a training seminar for native pastors, the rest of the team repaired the roof of a church building and constructed a small medical clinic. They returned home to Grace Church with exciting stories to tell, and their reports back to their congregation included many stories of the physical hardships they experienced, the poverty they witnessed, and what they had accomplished. The reported results of their short-term mission trip included the following:

- The 18 people who were sent experienced a powerful spiritual impact on their own lives. Three of the young people indicated that they felt called to full time ministry. The others testified to having their faith renewed and experiencing a closer walk with God.

- A church roof was repaired and a clinic was 80% constructed.

- The team members befriended a number of non-Christians and two of them prayed to receive Christ.

- Grace Church spent $29,000 on trip expenses for the team.

A Hispanic mission leader followed up with a visit to the area and discovered that, unknown to the team members, there were also some unreported results from their visit:

- Some of the Guatemalan Christian workers and leaders were encouraged to know that foreign Christians cared about them and were praying for them. Their spirits were lifted by friendships made with the American team members.

- Members of the church whose building was

repaired concluded that they did not need to give money or take responsibility for their building. They concluded that if the roof or some other part of the building ever needed repair again, some foreigners would come to do that. Three years later, the building seemed to be in worse shape than before the short-term trip.

- Some skilled Guatemalan craftsmen who could have worked on the building for a fraction of the cost incurred by the short-term team, remained unemployed during and after the trip.

- Non-Christians who observed the foreign activity and the English speaking visitors concluded that this particular church was a foreign brand of Christianity and perhaps not suitable for most people native to the region.

- The pastors attended the training seminars out of politeness and hope for future financial help, although they did not admit this to the short-term team members. One pastor said, "We had to sit through hours of boring lectures by foreign guest teachers, in order to secure a few precious resources that will come to us only if we allow the foreigners to have the stage."

- Of the two people who received Christ, one eventually joined the local church. The other one did not follow through and contact was lost with her.

Shortly after the team returned, the Mission Committee of Grace Church received a request for financial support from another evangelistic agency. This agency was reporting new disciples being won to Christ for a cost of only about $10 per convert, and in a country that is less than 2% Christian. In contrast, Guatemala is more than 50% Christian, and the short-term mission team resulted in converts at a cost of thousands of dollars per new disciple. Yet the committee was not able to provide additional funds to this agency due to the Grace Church policy of giving priority to their short-term mission teams.

Short-term Memories

The experience of the Grace Church short-term mission team is not unique. Short-term mission trips, even more than sending full-time missionaries, often serve primarily to minister to the workers rather than to the lost. Joanne Van Engen aptly sums up the hard reality: "North Americans spend millions of dollars each year on Missions/related trips to developing nations. Many of them do more harm than good."*

Ideally, the short-term team members return home with enthusiasm for the Great Commission and some understanding of what God is doing in far-away places. Hopefully, the participants will be stimulated to

---

* Joanne Van Engen, "The Cost of Short-term Missions," The Other Side, January 2000, p. 20.

become more involved in God's work outside their own community. But do they?

Unfortunately, some researchers say they don't. Some studies have concluded that the long-term impact of short-term mission trips is negligible, and perhaps even negative in terms of overall resources (people and money) going to missions. So often it seems that the impact of the short-term adventure dissipates quickly over time, and that the heavy investment of time and money into the short-term expenses does not produce the hoped-for impact.[†]

Measuring That Matters

Are we measuring our Great Commission impact? Or are we satisfied to field a team of enthusiasts and just hope for the best? It's not that short-term visits to a mission field are necessarily without value. Rather, we need to design and operate short-term experiences in a way that really focuses on the Great Commission results we claim to care about. This means holding up the ultimate objective, and following up the visit with a long-term plan to invest in that objective.

This means being brutally honest about what we have and have not accomplished for the Kingdom. In order to

---

[†] See Marshall Allen, "Missions Tourism?" *Faithworks*, October 1, 2000: www.faithworks.com/archives/mission_tourism.html; K. VerBeek, 2002 Unpublished paper: "The Impact of Short-term Missions": www.calvin.edu/academic/sociology/staff/kurt.htm; T. Purvis, *Partnerships in Cross-cultural Missions*, 1993; Randy Friesen, "Long-term impact of short-term missions," *Evangelical Missions Quarterly*, October 2005; Laura Montgomery, "Short-Term Medical Missions," *Missiology* 21:3, July 1993.

help us do that, we need to be able to calculate the spiritual return on our investments, whether that be a short-term trip, an overseas missionary, or a financial donation.

Especially during times of extremely fast church growth, foreign missionaries and their finances can actually "get in the way" and block growth unless they carefully consider the outcome of their assistance and the limitations of their role. There is danger in sending money as well as sending short-term mission teams. The Western church has had centuries of experience in trying to finance overseas ministries, and has made many tragic mistakes along the way. Well-intentioned but naïve churches provide many gifts of cash, buildings, educational opportunities, and materials. But all too often these not only fail to achieve the objective to advance the Kingdom of God, but can actually result in significant set-backs for the Gospel.

Nearly a century has passed since people like John L. Nevius, Roland Allen, and Melvin Hodges supplied us with the principles that they learned for fostering healthy indigenous movements through financial abstinence.[‡] These men and others like them have supplied us with a rich library of reflections on the experiences of thousands of Great Commission workers in the late 19th century and early 20th century. Yet today, in complete ignorance of those lessons, many well-meaning Western believers

‡ See for instance, Allen's *Missionary Methods: St Paul's or Ours?*

persist in enabling needy churches or their leaders with destructive financing. The negative impact of Western finances is so widespread and its results so pernicious that many informed missiologists and national church leaders actually applaud governmental restrictions that prevent material assistance from flowing freely from West to East.

For instance, many church leaders in Mainland China, aware of the sad history of financial prostitution, pray earnestly that their authoritarian government will not change its policy that severely inhibits the attempts of Western churches to "help" the cause of Christ in China. In India, large indigenous mission agencies like Friends Missionary Prayer Band have built their ministry on the core value of refusing all assistance from abroad.

It's not that such assistance is inherently evil, but that those supplying assistance, as well as those receiving it, have often failed to consider the long-term impact of financial support on Great Commission objectives. Some have been carried away by their compassion for the "poor" without considering how they are affecting the spiritual outcomes for the cause of Christ. Missiologists learned long ago that permanent overseas financial support for a native worker always suppresses and limits what the national church can achieve for the Great Commission. Overseas financial investment in the construction of native church buildings always suppresses and limits the stewardship and vitality of the congregations who worship in those facilities. Long-term financial subsidy from overseas causes dependence, and dependence always short-circuits church growth.

It's not that all financial help is bad. There is a way to use Western finances to advance the Gospel in non-Western societies. The kind, quantity, and manner of financial help needs to be carefully calculated for its effect on the making of new disciples, planting of churches, and potential for explosive growth of the Kingdom that we all desire. One must thoroughly submit all plans to these over-riding objectives, allowing them to over-rule any assumptions about how to use money to advance the Great Commission.

The remedy for distraction is likewise measuring our progress. But keeping count is not easy. It's easier to just stay busy with lots of activities, or to finance pet projects and just "leave the results to God." Dismissively leaving the results to God can just be an excuse for a lack of passion and follow-through.

{ 5

Great Commission Passion

As a high school student, I participated in debate and forensics competitions, representing Battle Creek Central High School. Coach James Copeland demanded a lot from us. We practiced every single day after school. Practically every Saturday during the school year, and many weeks during summer vacation, we were on the road attending various speaking and debating tournaments.

If anyone complained about the demanding schedule, Coach Copeland invited that person to leave the team. He sometimes quoted a nationally known football coach who was still in his prime back in those days: "Winning is not the most important thing. It's the only thing." Copeland interpreted this motto as follows: "Winning means that you have learned more than the other guy, that you have gained more skills than the other guy, that you are more capable today than you were yesterday. It's an indication of accomplishment. Since we are here to learn as much as we can, we are going to keep track of wins and losses. And we are going to focus on winning."

Copeland was passionate about high school forensics. He later became Executive Director of the National

Forensics League. His passion was contagious. We worked our hearts out, and our high school forensics team won most tournaments we entered, including First Place in the National Forensics League championship tournament in Albuquerque New Mexico in 1966. Needless to say, we all learned a lot—and I never forgot his passion.

Passion for Pastoring

During my first term in the Philippines, I was responsible for a church planting effort in the small rural town of Murcia. The congregation was composed of about 100 people who met for worship under a thatched roof, with a dirt floor and no walls. The families were typical of the community, composed mostly of poorly paid sugar cane workers and their families. Many of the members were single women, of which there were a high percentage in Murcia. Their husbands had either died, or had abandoned their families to seek a new life elsewhere.

The undisputed leader of the church was elder Digno Patilla. This short, grizzly, 60-year-old fish vendor got up every morning at 3:00 a.m. to take the long ride down to the fishing docks in the nearby city of Bacolod. There he would purchase fresh fish from the one-man fishing boats as they came in from their night's work and then take the long ride back to Murcia. By sun-up, without fail, he would be walking up and down the narrow alley-ways in Murcia shouting, "Isda, Isda" (*fish, fish*). Many people started their day with a breakfast of fresh fish, and Digno served them well. By 9:30 or 10:00 a.m., his work day was done.

That's when Digno really got to work. Before noon, he was visiting with one of the church's families. Usually this meant hiring a motorized tricycle to take him out into the sugar cane fields. Most families lived in one-room nipa huts, raised on stilts with split-bamboo floors and often without one piece of furniture. This was not so different from Digno's own house in the town, except that Digno had a table and two chairs. Digno would shout his greeting as he approached, climb up into the hut, and squat on the floor for a friendly conversation with whatever adult was present. After opening with polite exchanges, Digno quickly got around to the purpose of his visit. "Have your children eaten anything recently? Do you have any food in the house? Is anyone sick?"

If the children had eaten something within the past 24 hours and no one was sick, then everything was well. But often the kids had eaten nothing for a day or two. If this was the case, Digno would dig into his shoulder bag, pull out a small plastic bag of rice, and offer it to Mom or Dad. He would then lead them in a prayer of thanks and ask for God's blessing on the household.

Digno would then go on to the next house. By late afternoon, he would be back home for a light supper and bed in preparation for tomorrow's early morning wake-up. This was Digno's daily schedule. Digno's travels took him through territory controlled by the New People's

Army, an armed Maoist insurgency that was mobilizing the victims of the brutal poverty that saturated Murcia and the surrounding areas. Digno told me, "We know who these people are. We don't go out after dark. But we are not afraid of them and for the most part they respect us."

I was present when the pastor of a neighboring church that was supervising their ministry was meeting with Digno and the other leaders of the church in Murcia. The pastor asked, "Are you visiting the members of your church in their homes?"

Answering for the group, Digno nodded.

The pastor asked, "How often do you visit with the members in their homes?"

Digno said, "Every two weeks."

The pastor said, "No, I mean, how often do you visit all members in their homes?"

Digno said, "Yes, every two weeks. I visit every member at least once every two weeks. I go out every day to do this. We are happy to do this because our members need our help and our prayers."

Digno was truly a happy and contented man. I never heard him complain. I never heard him criticize. Could this be because he had a shepherd's passion that consumed his waking moments?

Biblical Passion for Winning

There is no greater demand for passion than the Great Commandment: "Love the Lord your God with all your heart and with all your soul and with all your strength" (Deut. 6:4; Matt. 22:36-37). Jesus Christ wants passionate followers. He is not satisfied with mediocrity or half-hearted "don't-care-if-we win" team members. His business is taking losers and turning them into passionate winners.

Of course, Jesus' definition of "winning" and "losing" is very different than the world's definition. Winning Jesus' way does not mean cutting down or dominating other people. Jesus' definition of winning actually requires more passion than the world demands of its competitors:

"Anyone who does not carry his cross and follow me cannot be my disciple . . . any of you who does not give up everything he has cannot be my disciple" (Luke 14:27, 33).

The greatest church planter in the New Testament was known for his incredible passion. Paul's passion was seen in the long list of intense sufferings that he endured for the cause of Christ (2 Cor. 6:3-10; 11:16-33). He explained the believer's passion in terms of winning an athletic contest. "Do you not know that in a race all the runners run, but only one gets the prize? Run in such a way as to get the prize . . . I do not run like a man running aimlessly; I do not fight like a man beating the air. No, I beat my body and make it my slave so that after I have preached to others, I myself will not be disqualified for the prize" (1 Cor. 9:24, 26-27).

Paul made it clear that his suffering was not just a religious exercise intended for his own spiritual benefit. He intended to win, and he urged others to do the same.

His passion was focused on winning the race, a race with observable objectives.

> Now I rejoice in what I am suffering for you, and I fill up in my flesh what is still lacking in regard to Christ's afflictions, for the sake of his body, which is the church . . . to make known among the Gentiles the glorious riches of this mystery, which is Christ in you, the hope of glory. He is the one we proclaim, admonishing and teaching everyone with all wisdom, so that we may present everyone mature in Christ. To this end I strenuously contend [Greek connotation: agonize], with all the energy Christ so powerfully works in me (Col. 1:24, 27-29).

Paul asked the same commitment of the members of the early church: "Offer your bodies as living sacrifices . . . Then you will be able to test and approve what God's will is" (Rom. 12:1-2). Paul did not have a martyr complex, nor did he have a passion to suffer. He had a passion to please Christ by accomplishing the goal that Christ had given him, and therefore to marshal every resource to achieve that objective.

Captivating Thoughts

In his book, *Winning on Purpose*,* John Kaiser applies this

---

*Abingdon Press, 2006.

principle to the ministry of a local church. He says that the foundation of every church's purpose is Jesus' marching orders in the Great Commission (p. 52). The application is even more relevant to the mission field. A suffering 21st century missionary is following Paul's example when she is suffering with passion for the Great Commission objectives that fueled Paul's life.

If we are really passionate for that objective, then we will do everything possible to achieve it. In the same way that the Apostle Paul sought to "take captive every thought to make it obedient to Christ" (2 Cor. 10:5), the apostles of the 21st century seek to take captive every mental tool in order to serve the cause of Christ with every ounce of energy and every human ability that He has given us. God has given us numbers and measures. The ability to keep score is a mental tool worth using for the cause of Christ: "God has founded all things—number, weight, and measure" (Isaac Newton).

If we are really striving with all of the energy that God gives us, and focusing all of God's gifts on the task we have received, then it is not enough to work without noting or reporting the results. God has given us numbers and measures, and God expects us to use them.

The determination to use numbers and measures will cost something, especially for Great Commission ministries that are targeting people groups that are still unreached. Two agencies I have worked with, Bible League and Mission India, invest a significant portion of their ministry resources in the staff and reporting systems needed to keep track of measurable ministry results.

In the case of India for instance, monitoring and reporting ministry results is the primary focus of the in-country staff of Mission India (numbering 406 at this writing). In order to receive Mission India resources, potential partnering organizations in India must demonstrate two things:

(1) a passion for church planting on a large, visionary scale; and

(2) a willingness to report.

The first requirement is an indication that the church or agency is passionate about the right objective. The second requirement is an indication of the depth of their determination to make an impact for Christ. All of this is a direct result of Mission India's determination to implement its mission statement to "assist Indian churches and indigenous mission agencies in planting reproducing churches in a systematic and measurable way."

Thankfully, the Holy Spirit has given India a disproportionate number of extremely passionate workers. Mission India and India's Gospel workers have become passionate about measuring what matters because they are already passionate about following Christ and His Great Commission. To a great extent, William Carey's motto is in the spiritual genes of the church in India: "Attempt great things for God. Expect great things from God."

What are the great things? How do we know if we have achieved them or received them?

It is difficult or impossible to be passionate, transparent, or accountable for results unless you are measuring the great things done for God.

{ 6

Measuring Spiritual Returns on Investment

For-profit companies keep score with their "bottom line," commonly referred to as "return on investment," which is usually focused on profit margin. Profit margins have become so universally dominant in evaluating the success or failure of a business that some business analysts are now warning that the company bottom line must be expanded to include non-financial metrics for multiple stake-holders, as in the system being taught by Robert Kaplan at Harvard Business School called "The Balanced Scorecard." * Businesses have learned that measuring only finances is not enough. There are other important measures that can indicate the relative health of a company or business. Whatever your business, it is important to identify what your bottom line is, and then to use your bottom line results to evaluate and improve your performance.

In order to make the best use of limited ministry resources, we need to work within a similar paradigm—one that I refer to as SROI: Spiritual Return on Investment. It's a way of measuring what matters in the great battle.

---

* See the book by the same title.

Although I developed the SROI model independently of the "Social Return on Investment" model advocated by Dale Galvin,[†] his concerns parallel mine: too many social service organizations are characterized by a lack of metrics and lack of accountability for their outcomes.

"If you don't know what kind of difference you are making you will be forever confused. You won't know how to allocate resources. You won't have a framework to make day-to-day decisions. And you won't know when you have won" (p. 38).

The City of Baltimore, for instance, concluded that "if you're not measuring it, you're not managing it" and instituted a "government by numbers" program that resulted in remarkable improvements in the city's battles with urban problems. As a result, the number of Baltimore school children who tested positive for lead poisoning was reduced by 80%, and for the first time potholes in city streets are now being fixed within 48 hours. These improvements were due to the transparency that comes from comprehensive measuring of the service objectives of various city departments.[‡]

We Christians also need to measure how effectively we are participating in the spiritual battle. The SROI

[†] "Tiny Bubbles: A Guide to the New Non-Profit Economy," *Nonprofit Quarterly*, Summer 2006, pp. 32ff.

[‡] Noah Weiss, "Government by Numbers," *Stanford Social Innovation Review*, Winter 2007, p. 68

paradigm for mission agencies measures success by "spiritual return on investment." Investment includes money, time, and prayers, whether by paid staff, donors, or volunteers who have committed themselves to accomplish the mission. The "spiritual" return is defined by the organization's particular mission and objectives. Whether you are an individual believer or a Christian organization, you are investing in God's future, and you can define the spiritual returns on your investments.

Standard of Measure

The most significant spiritual returns in terms of the Great Commission are new "disciples made" and new "churches planted." New disciples and new churches are the focus of the Book of Acts, and have been the strategic focus of nearly every Great Commission mission agency since the New Testament. Two Scripture texts among the many that spell out these objectives are:

- Matthew 28:19: "make disciples of all nations." The word "go" is not the command of this passage; the word of command in this verse is "make disciples." Disciples are individuals who show by their words and actions that they have committed their lives to following the teachings and commands of Jesus. *Ethne*, the Greek word for "nations," refers not to the geo-political countries as we conceive them, but rather to "ethnic groups" or "people groups." There are about 16,000 known people groups in our world, of which nearly 7,000 are still considered to be unreached by the Gospel because there are so few disciples in them.[*] In that context, consider the SROI question: How successfully are we investing to reach these unreached people groups, and to make disciples of all people groups?

- Revelation 7:9: "there before me was a multitude that no one could count, from every nation, tribe, people and language." The innumerable multitude of disciples in John's vision represents individual converts and also represents every people group on earth. The SROI question: To what extent do our mission investments serve to populate the multitude of disciples around the throne of God?

Poor Stewardship

While most churches and Great Commission agencies say that they want to make disciples and start new churches, very few actually measure, evaluate, and report their impact based on these measures. Very few it seems are keeping count.

In a for-profit company the ratio of return to investment is a straightforward formula, because ordinarily both measures in the equation are dollars, easily calculated

---

[*] "Gospel Progress Levels," accessed February 13, 2012, http://www.joshuaproject.net/global-progress-scale.php

as one divided by the other. In a Great Commission ministry, one way to measure a meaningful spiritual return on investment will be the ratio of dollars spent to the number of new disciples made, or the ratio of dollars spent to the number of new churches planted.

The SROI paradigm reasons, *If I am convinced that God has entrusted dollars into my bank account so that I can invest those dollars in obedience to the Great Commission, then it is incumbent on me to invest them as wisely as possible, with the best return I can manage.*

Jesus' parables of the *minas* (Luke 19:11-27) and the *talents* (Matt. 25:14-30) reveal that God gives rewards based on return on investment. The lazy investor, or the selfish investor, or the investor who does not have his Master's priorities in mind, will gain a lower return on his investment than the faithful investor who wants to give his very best for the Master, to please his Master, and to achieve his Master's objectives.

Ideally, my SROI will tell me what it cost me for each disciple made last year, and how many dollars were spent for each new church that was established. How many workers were fielded, how many prayers offered, and how many dollars spent to achieve these results? I should be able to compare the relative cost to make a disciple in the central Indian state of Madhya Pradesh with the cost in southern Tamil Nadu. Those who know India well will guess that the cost is higher in Madhya Pradesh because the harvest is not as plentiful there. Enemy forces are stronger in Madhya Pradesh.

Number Power

Scorekeepers will also discover, however, that the spiritual
return on investment is much higher everywhere in India
than in most other nations on earth because the Holy
Spirit is preparing hearts in both Tamil Nadu and Madhya
Pradesh to receive Christ as never before in India's history.

Does this mean that the church today should be
investing more resources in India? Most certainly! Jesus
told His disciples that when they met stubborn opposition,
they were to "shake the dust off of their feet" and move on
to the next village. Paul told his resistant Jewish listeners
that because they rejected the Gospel, therefore he would
turn to the Gentiles. And when Paul was meeting some
opposition from the population in Corinth, the Lord
appeared to him in a dream and ordered him to persevere
in his work in Corinth "because I have many people in this
city" (Acts 18:6-10).

Results matter to God, and they should matter to
us, even to the point of determining where and when we
invest the Lord's resources.

SROI can also determine how to invest the Lord's
resources. If most organizations working in a particular
region have a significant measurable SROI, and my
ministry does not, then I need to evaluate what I am doing
wrong. When a population is responsive to the Gospel,
there is sometimes a greater response to one evangelistic

method than to other methods. In a for-profit company, if you are far less efficient and effective than your competitors who are working in the same market-place, you will eventually go bankrupt. You must figure out what you can do better. Why should Great Commission ministries not do the same?

Measuring the difference you are making requires numbering. As long as there have been people seeking to increase their significance and to multiply their impact, there have been people who discovered the power of numbering.

All Christian ministries are made up of significant countable outputs and countable outcomes, including countable people. There is nothing particularly spiritual about not counting them. A numerical approach to accountability is in accord with God's will as revealed in the Scriptures. Numerical accountability can be a powerful tool to help people be good stewards of God's resources.

{ 7

The Power of Numbers

The power of numbering begins with the power of "one." Whether or not you do it with discipline and forethought, every person and every organization constantly measures things, and most often the measure is "one." A Bible translator writes her victory letter to the churches and individuals who have been supporting her for the past 15 years, praising God that her New Testament is complete and ready for the publisher. She does not write "one New Testament" completed (as opposed to two or three). But she could do so if she chose.

A missionary reports to his sending board that a leading Muslim in his city has accepted Christ and been baptized. He tells the story of the man's initial hostility and skepticism, followed by cautious curiosity, Bible study, and first prayers to Issa (the Arabic name for Jesus). He describes the outrage of his fellow Muslims and threats from the man's family. He does not say "one Muslim has entered the Kingdom of God" (as opposed to two or three or a hundred). But he could say that if he chose. In fact, if Muslims are normally baptized by the dozens or hundreds, he might report, "In City X, only one was baptized."

Counting is important because "one" is important. When there is more than one thing to count, counting does not reduce their value. Rather, choosing to count something is an indicator of value. In many cases, the problem is that numbers are disconnected from their context, or those who hear the numbers do not understand their referents. The church of which I am a member lists 336 professing members. Without me, the number would be 335. Or if I bring a new member into the congregation, the number will grow to 337. If you belong to a much larger congregation, you might not be impressed by such numbers. But from my personal point of view, there is a huge qualitative difference between 335 and 337.

What do numbers do? How do numbers apply to Christian ministry? Is it accidental that the Greek root of the English word "mathematics" is the same word that Jesus used as His central command in the Great Commission: *matheteusate*: "make disciples"? In English, "math" has come to mean "the study of quantity and magnitude of numbers." *

Can a true "disciple" ignore the "discipline of mathematics" in his service to Christ?

In keeping with the biblical perspective, numbers do several things: make our vision concrete, give the big picture, and help us make choices.

---

* Webster's Dictionary, 1993

Numbers Make Vision Concrete

We usually describe what God is doing or what He will do in general terms that serve to inspire and motivate others to praise Him or to take action in response to His commands. Such general statements of principle or vision are understood only when they become concrete in our lives or our world. It's easy to ignore a generality, but not so easy to ignore a very concrete command or description. Telling a story or giving a specific example is one way to make vision concrete. Describing with numbers also makes vision concrete.

One organization (DAWN Ministries) has promoted a worldwide vision to "see saturation church planting become the generally accepted and fervently practiced strategy for completing the task of making disciples of all peoples in our generation."[†] The theological basis of this vision is the New Testament mandate to plant churches in fulfillment of the Great Commission. This vision was made concrete in the Philippines in 1979 when most evangelical churches and missions agreed with DAWN to try to "establish 50,000 worshiping congregations by the year 2000," a goal which, if achieved, would effectively saturate the nation with churches.

When I first moved to the Philippines in 1976, you could have randomly visited any community there and the

---

[†] See James Montgomery, *DAWN 2000: 7 Million Churches to Go*, William Carey Library, 1989; and *Then the End Will Come*, William Carey Library, 1997

chances were only one in four that you would have found a Protestant church. Shortly after my arrival, I and several hundred other church and mission leaders met together, along with James Montgomery and Donald MacGavran, to strategize how to give legs to the DAWN vision. Although not a resident of the Philippines, MacGavran studied the numerical and narrative reports of the most active church planting missions and urged us to set an aggressive goal of establishing a church in every single community. When I asked him how we were going to do that, he said, "The evidence is clear. Those who promote small group Bible studies have found the secret to church planting in the Philippines. Multiply small groups." This worked.

Today, the chances of finding a church in any community are more than 80%, a result of partially achieving the vision that was realized as a numerical objective. Of the many Christian ministries in the Philippines that participated in this vision, those that were careful to measure their results were the ones that contributed the most to filling Filipino communities with churches.

When Peter referred to "the few" who were saved from the Flood, he thought it significant enough to specify "eight in all" (1 Peter 3:20). Not only Stephen the preacher, but also Luke the author of Acts, thought it important in telling the story of Jacob's family going down to Egypt to specify "seventy five in all" (Acts 7:14). When Mark contrasted the giving of the widow with the giving of the wealthy Pharisees, he could have stuck to generalities. Instead, he referred to the widow's "two very small copper coins" (Mark 12:42) to provide the concrete image for Jesus' teaching.

John reports that the miraculous catch of great fish totaled 153 fish in all, "but even with so many, the net was not torn" (John 21:11). Can it be that this post-resurrection miracle refers prophetically to the gathering in of the Gentiles, whom the rabbis believed were metaphorically represented by the varieties of fishes in the sea, believed at that time to total 153 distinct species of fish? It makes sense that the post-resurrection miracle would focus on the mission to the Gentiles, as compared to the earlier miraculous catch (Matt. 13:47-50 and Luke 5:8-10), performed before the disciples understood who Jesus was, much less what was His mission for them. In the earlier miracle, the nets tore, but in the Great Commission version, the nets miraculously held the great number of converts.

In Revelation 11:1, John was instructed to "count the worshipers" in order to demonstrate in a concrete way the triumph and magnitude of God's final victory and grace, and in a pastoral way to assure the protection of God's whole flock from the spiritual attacks that would soon assail them. The pastoral concern is also illustrated in the story of the man with a hundred sheep (Matt. 18:12-13), who could hardly have known that one was missing had he not counted them!

Numbers in the Bible, as elsewhere, give a specific concrete magnitude and shape to a general idea or vision.

Numbers Give the Big Picture

Numbers have the power to gather many specific accomplishments into a single big-picture summary.

Bob Hoskins, founder of Book of Hope International, was given a Spirit-led vision for a child that he saw on a playground—a passion that this child would be delivered from demonic attacks.[‡] Later he saw Book of Hope answer his prayers for 9-year-old Tiffany living in Peru. Numbers now tell him that Book of Hope has been delivered to over 20 million such children in Brazil alone, and more than 250 million worldwide. It's wonderful to transform the life of a single 9-year-old child. It's more wonderful yet to know how the lives of millions are touched.

The theological validity of transforming the life of a 9-year-old child through the Word of God is easy to demonstrate. Anyone who reads the story of Tiffany understands not only a little bit more about Bob Hoskins' passion, but something about the way the Holy Spirit is at work. The numbers extend that understanding to the big picture.

Fifty years ago, another 9-year-old boy, J. Chiranjeevi, wandered into a church in central India that was conducting a daily vacation Bible school. As a result, his

---

[‡] Hoskins, *Affect Destiny*, pp. 7-8, and p. 75.

life was transformed by Christ. His spirit was inspired by a vision to bring the same transformation to 300 million children in India. Today, he is able to measure 4 million boys and girls each year that are touched by the Children's Bible Clubs of Mission India, and last year alone, 2.4 million children were transformed just as his life was. He is determined to reach the hundreds of millions who are still waiting to be touched by Jesus. Faithful numbering tells him how far along God is in fulfilling the vision that He has given Chiranjeevi.

The same interweaving of individual transformation and numerical summaries is found in the Book of Acts. You can find the individual impact of the Gospel in the lives of some persons who shouted, "Brothers, what shall we do?" (Acts 2:37), or in the life of a single crippled beggar (Acts 3:1-10), a Levite from Cyprus named Joseph (Acts 4:32-36), those tormented by evil spirits (Acts 5:16), Samaritans (Acts 8:4-8), an Ethiopian (Acts 8:36-39), or Aeneas and Dorcas (Acts 9:32-41). These individual portraits of impact are expanded into the "big picture perspective" by the references in Acts to "three thousand" baptized (Acts 2:41), "those added to their number" (Acts 2:47), "five thousand men" (Acts 4:4), "more and more men and women added to their number" (Acts 5:14), "the number of disciples increasing" (Acts 6:1), "a large number of priests obedient to the faith" (Acts 6:7), and many references to the church "growing in numbers" and "increasing" (Acts 9:31, 42; 11:21; 12:24; 14:21,27;

16:5). The combination of detailed individual stories and numerical summaries paints a portrait of the nature and extent of God's transforming power in the early church.

The Gospels portray Jesus' ministry in a similar manner. The disciples learned faith in Jesus the miracle-worker who showed His power to feed or water a few people, as He did in John 2 in fulfillment of the Messianic prophecies of Amos 9:11-15. But could they trust Him to feed the families of 5,000 men with only 5 small loaves, 2 small fish, and 12 resulting baskets of leftovers? The contrasting numbers take the individual impacts and extend them into a big picture discovery: "Surely this is the Prophet" (John 6:14).

To this day, virtually all of the world's 36,400 distinct Christian denominations have followed the model of Acts 2 by baptizing, enumerating, and recording their baptized memberships. And research shows that "most react strongly to disparaging or critical assessments of their censuses from outside."[§] More than anything, Christian denominational leaders value their individual members. If given enough time, they could describe them one-by-one, at least the ones they know personally. They summarize and extend this value by enumerating the total body of believers within their fellowships.

In the same research, David Barrett reports that

---

§ David Barrett, "Annual Statistical Table," *International Bulletin of Missionary Research*, Vol. 27, No. 1, January 2003, page 24.

whenever the Devil sneered at Martin Luther's wavering hope of personal salvation, Luther would rush to his study and scrawl in chalk *"Baptizatus sum"* rather than *"Conversus sum"* as some of his fellow Reformers would have preferred. When used properly, numbers represent something observable, not mere human opinion. This is why Barrett the statistician lifts up "baptized members" as the most important category of Christian measurement: this category of people is almost universally significant to all parts of the Church, and the measure is based on observable human behavior, not supposition or opinion.

Every number starts with "one." What does one "baptized member" look like? Can you describe him? Would you know one if you saw one? Presumably, you would know one if you saw her at the instant of her baptism.

Some organizations measure "commitments," "converts," or "decisions." But what does a commitment look like? What behavior guarantees that a person can be called a "commitment"? Presumably there is a behavioral element behind claims to measure decisions, converts, or commitments to Christ. Perhaps these are people who orally prayed something called "the sinner's prayer"? Or perhaps these people raised their hands above their heads after a showing of the Jesus Film? Or perhaps they got up out of their chairs and walked to the front of an auditorium? Or perhaps they said "Yes" when another person asked them the question, "Do you accept Jesus as your personal Lord and Savior?" Or perhaps they stood in front of a firing squad and met death rather than denounce their Lord?

Numbers are most helpful when they represent a common category of observed behavior or observable phenomenon.

Great Commission impact is about making disciples. Counting becomes important when observable events have multiplied to the point where it is impossible to understand how or to what extent disciples are being made just by incidental observation or mental arithmetic. Webster's defines quantification as "the transformation of qualitative into quantitative data," which Barrett compares to placing mile-markers along a highway to enable travelers to assess their progress.** Barrett lists 23 Greek imperative verbs that have unique English translations clearly instructing the listener or reader of the Scriptures to "count something" related to obeying the Great Commission.†† Church leaders who are concerned about the "all nations" (*panta ta ethne*) of the Great Commission can hardly ignore the enormous complexity of our world, with its 7 billion humans grouped in thousands of ethno-linguistic peoples. This size and complexity requires not less but more disciplined numbering.

** David B. Barrett and Todd M. Johnson, *World Christian Trends* (Pasadena, California: William Carey Library, 2001), p. 463.

†† Ibid. p. 448.

Numbers Help Us Choose

Numbers in the Bible sometimes provide the reasons for choices. God chose Gideon, among "the weakest" of his tribe, to save Israel from the Midianites. In order to fulfill His purpose "that Israel may not boast against me," God further instructed Gideon how to reduce the size of his army from the original 32,000 volunteers, to 22,000, and then further to only the 300 warriors chosen by God to deliver Israel from Midian (Judges 6-7). This small band routed an enemy army of 120,000 swordsmen. Usually we choose bigger numbers to maximize impact. In this case, God chose smaller numbers for the same purpose.

King Saul thought that the people were choosing David over him because of the people's song, "Saul has slain his thousands and David his ten thousands" (1 Sam. 18). Abraham's intercessions for Sodom (Gen. 18) were based on his hope that the number of godly residents (from 50, to 45, to 40, to 30, to 20, to 10) would convince God to choose to spare the city from destruction. And God implied to Jonah that the 120,000 people in Nineveh "who cannot tell their right hand from their left" were the reason for God's decision to spare the city from destruction (Jonah 4:11).

Jesus clearly commanded His followers to reach all *ethne*. How can we determine which populations have yet to be reached; that is, which are most neglected relative to the Great Commission? India provides an instructive example. Great Commission organizations like Mission India have strategized for years how to deploy limited resources into the second most populous nation on earth, arguably the one country most in need of such resources. Because the ministry of Mission India depends entirely on reliable national church partners, the "demand" for resources has come mostly from Kerala and Tamil Nadu, states with relatively higher percentages of Christians in the population (19.3% and 6.1% Christian respectively).

It would be easiest to work in these more Christian states. Yet the smaller relative numbers of Christians in the rest of India has led Mission India to make the extraordinary effort necessary to deploy resources equally in less responsive states. This means a purposed choice was made: assigning church planting resources into the unreached states of northern India (where the average number of Christians is less than 0.5%) even though it is much more difficult to find reliable partners in those regions.

8

Measuring What Matters

When Haregewoin Teferra, a middle-class Ethiopian woman, lost her husband and oldest daughter, she retreated into solitary mourning and despaired of life. Then one day she reluctantly agreed to take two AIDS orphans into her home. Directing her energy and attentions to them, she soon found new purpose in her life, sparking a life mission that transformed her home into a refuge for hundreds of orphans. A "nice neighborhood lady," she brought nothing unique to her effort except a purposeful motivation that enabled her to overcome incredible obstacles.

Haregewoin's modest household grew to seven children, then 18, then 42, until so many children crowded together, sleeping in tiny bedrooms and overflowing into the backyard in converted boxcars, that Haregewoin could hardly keep track of all of them. No one else would take them. So every night, Haregewoin crawled into her own bed that was already occupied by any number of tiny children. She impoverished herself caring for them, and yet at the same time, experienced joy and energy that became an inspiration to thousands.

Award winning journalist Melissa Fay Greene

documented Haregewoin's story and after years of research concluded, "I had to learn…You don't have to be a saint to rescue other people from suffering and death. You can just be an everyday, decent enough sort of regular person, nothing extraordinary, and yet turn lives around." [*] Haregewoin had the gift of focus—she measured what mattered in her life.

Measuring What Matters

Great Commission Christians need to measure what matters. When you begin measuring what matters most to God, you open up new ways to personal fulfillment and new ways to praise and glorify Him. The Great Commission is likely to become the "Great Completion" when we get serious about measuring the spiritual outcomes that need to characterize our ministries.

A well known organization is famous for organizing mass crusades where world-famous evangelists present the Gospel to thousands of people. They do their best to calculate their SROI by measuring what matters to them. Every year they report the number of "decisions made" for Christ, and tell the stories of some people who made those decisions. Over the past few years they have reported decisions costing as much as $5,800 per "decision made for Christ" and as little as $107 per decision. They also reported that their "decisions" were not necessarily

---

[*] *No Me without You*, page 481.

"disciples made" because as many as 60% of decisions were re-commitments of existing Christians. For a Great Commission advocate, the downside of their attempts to measure outcomes is that this organization has never reported whether the people making decisions actually end up as new disciples in the New Testament sense.

A better attempt to measure SROI typifies the annual reporting by one of the largest missionary sending agencies in the world. They reported new disciples made in their overseas ministries in the developing world at a cost of $395 per disciple after one recent year, and $613 per disciple in another recent year. They also reported new churches started in their overseas ministries at an average cost of $13,578 per new church.

Some non-sending mission agencies that channel resources only to national workers also report SROI. One very effective agency reported a worldwide average cost in 2005 of $5,648 (donated dollars) per new church planted, and $67 per "new church member." For the same year, Mission India reported an average SROI of $653 per new church planted and $4.42 per "new disciple."

Measuring Phases

Beware of comparisons. Because spiritual returns measure people, rather than dollars, simple comparisons are not always helpful. One agency report covered their ministries in 50 countries, while Mission India reported their ministries in India only. Regardless of which agency is reporting, the SROI in a place like Saudi Arabia is bound to be much lower than the SROI in India or the Philippines, even when the same ministry is using the same methods in each country. Some resources must still be invested in places like Saudi Arabia or the vision of Revelation 7:9 cannot be fulfilled.

To explain the differences in SROI, Mission India Founder John DeVries has compared the mission process to that of a new business venture. In phase one, a new business will typically require heavy financial investment without profits. In the current green energy industry in the USA, for instance, new businesses must be willing to invest for years without turning a profit in order to get established. The hope is that eventually, the base of loyal customers will reach a critical mass so that profits can be realized. Those who cannot tolerate years of deficit spending should stay out of the green energy business.

Phase two is when the successful business begins to make money. The business model proves itself by turning a profit. Investors can be wooed by reports of current earnings, and not merely future projections.

DeVries points out that there is sometimes a third phase in a business development, the one that entrepreneurs dream about, when the business "takes off" like a self-propelled rocket. The business no longer needs to "push" its product on wary customers. Rather, demand is such that potential customers are "pulling" for products or services that they desire, seeking out these products or services to such an extent that the business now has trouble meeting demand. This happens when so many people want to install your solar panels or purchase your electric car that your capacity is strained and you have difficulty meeting the demand.

On the mission field, Phase One can be compared to the initial efforts of cross-cultural missionaries to establish a spiritual beachhead. The going is rough. The converts are few. People are resistant to the weak efforts of foreigners. With modest results, missionaries are laying the foundation for later growth. In most contexts, this stage takes decades of persistent foot-slogging ministry.

Phase Two marks the point where new churches and the Gospel message begin to make real headway. Churches are growing steadily. With the help of cross-cultural missionaries, national leaders are being trained. During phase two, indigenous church leaders join the missionaries in ministry, and new churches begin to take ownership for reaching their own country with the Gospel.

Phase Three is marked by spontaneous expansion, as new disciples and new congregations seem to spring up everywhere. The Gospel is not so much being "pushed" on the uninterested—rather those who need the Gospel are "pulling" it in. People are ready to believe. This usually happens after a thorough indigenization of the message and the church structures, so that the target population no longer sees Christianity as a foreign intrusion. Growth is by multiplication rather than addition. Donald McGavran, formerly a missionary in India, described this as the time of great "people movements" for Christ.[†]

Twenty-first century missions is more and more characterized by phase three situations in which the Gospel is expanding exponentially. During the last 40 years of the twentieth century, the churches in the traditional "receiving countries" of the non-western world have grown more than ten times over. Non-western believers now outnumber western Christians by a factor of two-to-one, and the trend is still accelerating.[‡]

The astounding growth of the church in the Global South has intensified the issue of what role Western missionaries should have in Great Commission strategies. In my case for instance, if I were asked to return to the Philippines to once again live and work there as a foreign missionary, I would have to consider carefully whether there is any suitable role for me there. It's no accident that the agency that first sent me to the Philippines more than 40 years ago has reduced the number of missionaries they support in that country. Filipinos are now filling roles that were once assigned to foreign missionaries.

There are still locations where some kind of foreign missionary presence is needed. Saudi Arabia, for instance, is still a phase one situation, even though it is impossible to implement the traditional western sending model for

---

[†] See McGavran's classic book, *Understanding Church Growth.*

[‡] See for instance: Philip Jenkins' book, The Next Christendom.

this country. For political and cultural reasons, the foreign missionary role in Saudi Arabia will most likely best be filled by a non-western person, a Filipino or Indian for instance. George Patterson and Galen Currah[§] point out that the cross-cultural witnessing challenge is particularly difficult for most westerners as compared to non-western people, because conversions to Christ in Africa and Asia occur in the context of:

1. prayers for healing, rather than doctrinal preaching;
2. the influence of a brand new believer, rather than a professional worker or long-time Christian;
3. family decisions, rather than individualistic conversions; and
4. deep relationships with others in small group interactions where people are following the "one another" commands of the New Testament, rather than mass meetings or large congregations.

For cultural reasons, the churches of Africa and Asia generally already place a high priority on the values underlying these four aspects of ministry. For this reason, they are especially well suited to producing workers who are already skilled in these areas. Gospel workers who grow up and are educated in a western culture must overcome the immaturity and unbiblical values of western

§ *MentorNet #41*: "Witnessing for Christ in Other Cultures", 2006.

culture to be effective in these areas.

When Measuring Goes Wrong

As explained in the last chapter, numbers have their powerful uses. They also have their abuses. When someone derisively concludes, "We are not after numbers," they are usually reacting to an abusive use of measurements. Wrong measuring usually happens when the numbers or measures become disconnected from reality, or misaligned with the purpose of an activity.

Regardless of the kind of missionary sent, one cannot really compare the SROI for Saudi Arabia with the SROI for a radically different phase three country like the Philippines or India. Comparisons become meaningful when applied to like situations.

For instance, if a congregation or individual feels called to reach out to the Marathi people of North India, an unreached people group numbering in the tens of millions, then they would be wise to consider whether India is a phase one, a phase two, or a phase three situation. They should study carefully all of the alternative ways to reach the Marathi. Some current ministries to the Marathi are establishing new churches at a cost of less than $1,000 per new congregation. Others are spending tens of thousands of dollars among the Marathi with few disciples made and no new churches established.

The point is this: are you measuring what matters? You must discern whether it is good stewardship to invest your dollars with a person or organization that is accomplishing little. Could you be a better steward by empowering those who are accomplishing much?

But others might ask, *Why invest more in Saudi Arabia when you can invest in India?* Comparisons of SROI can help Great Commission Christians decide how and whom to target with their resources. Spiritual returns in Korea during the 19th century (phase one) were very different than the spiritual fruit experienced in the 1950s (phase three). The spiritual opportunities in North India during the 1950s cannot begin to compare with the opportunities today. Stubborn resistance has given way to responsive openness.

The work of the Holy Spirit sometimes presents a window of openness that may last for only a few years or a few decades. Due to political trauma, the decade of the 1990s was a period of great church growth for countries within the orbit of the former Soviet Union. SROI was high in Russia, Central Asia, and the Balkans. Since then, the work of disciple-making and church planting in this region has become more costly and less productive. It's important for Great Commission Christians to invest heavily and wisely during windows of responsiveness.

A focus on quantitative results is sometimes contrasted with a focus on qualitative results. "We are after quality, not quantity" is an implied criticism of measurements. What this generalization fails to acknowledge is that every quality can be measured. "To measure or not to measure" is not the issue. The issue is "what to measure."

Leaders of many of the fastest growing churches in America are learning that the "numerical size" of their congregations is not their ultimate objective. They are beginning to measure devotion, obedience, and inclusion. Depending on my church location and ministry goals, I might be more interested in how many people unlike me are feeling comfortable in my church or my small group rather than how many people are attending my church or my small group. I might decide that how many people worshiped with us last Sunday is less important than how many of last Sunday's worshipers are praying and reading the Bible every day.[**]

It all depends on what you define as your "spiritual returns." Measuring SROI will help make everyone aware of those responsive periods and places which otherwise might go unnoticed by those who think only in terms of sending a missionary or supporting a national worker. It will also help us to focus on what God has made most important as the desired outcome of our lives and ministries.

[**] For more on this, see Pat Springer, "The Benefits of Measuring Devotion and Obedience" www.leadnet.org; and Reveal: Where Are You? www.revealnow.com.

{ 9 }

Outputs and Outcomes

The Great Commission of Matthew 28:18-20 has a single Greek word of command (translated "make disciples") that describes the ultimate outcome that Jesus presents to His working followers. The outcome is disciples. There are also supporting activities found in the dependent clauses of those verses—words like "going" and "baptizing" and "teaching." These activities can also be described as objectives. As far as the Great Commission is concerned, they are objectives so long as they remain secondary to and supportive of disciple-making.

One can distinguish between the ultimate "outcomes" of a Great Commission ministry and the supporting activities that contribute to those outcomes. These supporting activities can be called "outputs" because they usually involve the investment of resources, time, and abilities that are more directly under our control.

In a manufacturing or service company, an output is usually the company's product. That can be anything—automobiles or electricity, for instance. The outcome can be described in various ways: satisfied drivers who purchase a car and drive comfortably and safely from one place to another, or residential home-owners who enjoy reliable and safe electricity in their homes at a reasonable price. In both of these examples, the ultimate outcome is a profit for the company.

In our personal lives, we can also distinguish between outputs and outcomes. If the duties of your 8-to-5 job are only an output, the outcome of which is your bi-weekly paycheck, then it doesn't matter so much whether you consider the job itself to be significant. For most workers, the paycheck is important, but not the only "outcome" by which they measure job satisfaction.

My work for the Bible League led me to Guangzhou, China, where a ministry partner had established a book-binding factory to facilitate the delivery of Chinese Bibles into the country. As with most factories at that time, the workers were almost entirely single women, ages 16-30, who had moved into the city from far away farming communities in order to earn money for their families back home. They worked six-day weeks, 12 hours per day. They slept and ate in crowded dormitories located on the factory grounds. Typically 80% of their paychecks were sent back home to Mom and Dad.

The factory manager explained that Sunday was a holiday, at that time unusual in Guangzhou; but this had become a problem because the young women went out and got part-time work to fill up their Sundays. He had intended Sunday to be a true day of rest for these hard working women, but for them, factory work was pure "output." They lived only for the "outcome" of sending the most money possible back home. His solution: the factory paid the workers a one-day "bonus" each week, on condition that they not seek additional employment for their day off. The result: a happier and more productive work force.

More to a Harvest than Planting Seeds

Life in the Spirit does not enslave us to unimportant outputs for the sake of all-important outcomes. Leading a small group prayer meeting is a spiritual "output" that in a Great Commission ministry hopefully will result in the "outcome" of committed disciples. Training a literacy worker, preaching a sermon, providing literature to a children's ministry, supporting a church planter—these all likewise are commendable activities that are the outputs of determined workers. They have great spiritual value in and of themselves, but they are not necessarily outcomes as far as accomplishing the Great Commission.

To use Jesus' own metaphor, we might compare such activities to the work that a farmer does in preparing the soil, sowing the seed, cultivating, fertilizing, sharpening the sickle (or tuning up the combine), and all of the other various activities that occupy the responsible farmer who is working hard for the greatest possible yield.

How deep did you plow? How many pounds of seed did you sow? How much herbicide and fertilizer did you use? What was the moisture content of the grain at the time of combining? These and other important activities can all be measured. The experienced farmer will tell you that there is a relationship between these measures and the ultimate outcome: bushels of grain harvested. All other things being equal, the right outputs will produce superior outcomes.

In the Philippines, our church planters were asked to measure, among other things, how many home Bible study groups they were leading. We discovered that there was a direct relationship between the number of home Bible study groups and the number of new disciples. We discovered that ongoing home Bible study groups often became new churches. A church planter could spin his wheels doing a lot of activities, some of which may have contributed to the planting of a church and some not. But the most important thing he needed to do, at the beginning at least, was to start small group home Bible studies. Church planters who did this succeeded. Church planters who neglected this failed.

In India, we ask our church planters to measure how many families they have visited and shared the Gospel with, how many prayer cells they have started, and how many Children's Bible Clubs organized, among other things. Given good soil already prepared by the Holy Spirit, such measures are good predictors of the harvest.

Prabhudas had been training with Mission India as a church planter in Andhra Pradesh for six months and reported 120 families visited and three prayer cells started. During the same time period, his classmate Murillo reported 400 families visited and six prayer cells started. Their different rates of outputs continued over the following year. It was no surprise to their mentor when, at the end of their two years of training, Prabhudas reported that one new church had been started, with 25 weekly worshipers, while Murillo reported three new churches with 70 new disciples worshiping weekly. The difference in outcomes was due not to a different responsiveness between the locations, but to a difference in outputs.

At the same time that Prabhudas and Murillo were learning how to plant churches, a pastor in a neighboring town, calling himself a church planter, did street preaching and did film presentations of Bible stories. He did not visit many people in their homes, and started no prayer cells. During the same two-year period, he was not able to establish a single new church.

Tactical Measurements

Measuring both outputs and outcomes can make a huge difference in the tactics being used by evangelists and disciple-makers. Most Great Commission ministries in India and the Philippines have discovered that mass crusades make no positive impact on church planting or disciple making objectives. In fact, mass crusades sometimes have a negative impact on such outcomes. Mass crusades are a very expensive ministry output that perhaps has some usefulness in some parts of the world, but not in these places.

An extensive survey of successful church planting ministries was conducted in India in 2003. One result that surprised many observers was the strong connection that emerged between ministries to children and new churches. It turned out that the majority of successful church planting ministries began with a ministry to Hindu or Muslim children. As researchers dug deeper into this phenomenon, it was discovered that children open doors into families that are otherwise resistant to evangelistic work. Ministries to children tend to build trust between the Christian workers and the community residents, and demonstrated in a practical way the loving concern of Christians for the families in the community. When operated right, ministries to children also influenced families through Gospel stories, Gospel songs, and habits of praying to Jesus.

Mission India's Children's Bible Clubs (CBCs) are being used all over India to open doors to evangelism in communities that would otherwise be closed to Gospel witness, including those areas of North India that have traditionally resisted Christian influence.

Mission India's record keeping of their activities and outcomes revealed some new information about how best to organize CBCs. Some CBCs were sponsored by churches that had a passion for church planting, while others were sponsored by churches with little or no vision for starting new churches. Some CBCs were modeled after vacation Bible schools and had an intensive ten-day summer program but no follow-up when the clubs ended. Other CBC sponsors followed up with "After School Clubs" in which the children came together every day during the school year. Careful score-keeping in regard to both outputs and outcomes of these various ministries led Mission India to two conclusions.

1. Children's Bible Clubs result in new churches only when the leaders of the church or agency who are in charge of the Club have a passion for church planting.

2. Children's Bible Clubs usually result in new churches when the clubs become "After School Clubs" that meet every day during the school year.

Since Mission India's desired outcome is new churches, it is important to know which outputs result in new churches. In order to maximize the church outcome, Mission India has learned to focus its outputs on the following: find local church or mission partners who already have a passion for starting new churches, and provide these partners with the training and materials they need in order to sponsor After School Children's Bible Clubs in neighborhoods that have no church. With this emphasis, new worshiping groups are now being planted in India at the rate of 11 new churches per day, using this youth-centric approach.

Measuring the Long-term

Even this measurable success is only a partial outcome. Mission India's mission is to help Indian Christians to establish reproducing churches. Are these 11 new churches being planted every day also going on to become reproducing churches? Answering that question with hard numbers is difficult and expensive because it involves long-term sustained contact with churches in tens of thousands of locations.

In this case, Mission India contracted another organization that specializes in research and asked them to discover whether churches established by its church planters are growing and reproducing after five years. Their conclusion: new churches have multiplied themselves three times over after their first five years of ministry.[*]

Effective mission agencies and individuals do not only "measure what matters" in the sense of measuring ultimate accomplishments. They also measure and hold themselves accountable for the outputs that are designed to achieve those accomplishments.

This is not easy. It is much easier to engage in favorite or enjoyable activities without regard for strategic outputs or ultimate outcomes. Staying focused requires discipline, and there is no better recipe for discipline than accountability.

---

[*] For more information, go to *www.metadigmgroup.com.*

{ 10

Accountability

Whether just starting up a business, or riding a wave of high demand and rapid growth, the responsible business leader not only keeps track of assets, liabilities, income and expenditures, but he or she also reports back to a board and investors, giving an account to them. Business leaders who are not transparent, who do not give an account to stock holders or board members, end up jobless or in legal trouble—and for good reason.

Have you ever been involved in a contest where the score-keeper was not doing the job? What a frustration. Or have you ever joined a game where the players said, *Let's just have fun, but not keep score?* I have. Sometimes it's fun. But it's not a real game. A team with that attitude is not a team that anyone could coach.

If you are involved in a life-or-death battle against a determined enemy, then not keeping track of how the battle is going, or not reporting that to others, is just not a rational option. In fact, under such circumstances, not being accountable for the outcomes of battle is a foolish dereliction of duty. You must assume that your enemy is measuring what matters!

Accounting for Spiritual Returns

Spiritual returns can be measured and accounted for, and there is a spiritual responsibility to do so. SROI can be measured and reported only if someone is accountable for measuring. Whether operating in a Phase One or Phase Three situation, Great Commission Christians need to give an account not only to God, but also to those who have invested time, prayers, and resources in their efforts. Accountability is not only a good business practice, but there is clear biblical precedence. Consider:

- Jesus' disciples reported back to Him when He sent them out on their mission (Luke 9:10; 10:17).
- The church planting teams in the Book of Acts reported back to those who sent them (Acts 14:27).
- The Master called his workers to account for everything that he had invested through their efforts (Matt. 25:14-30; Luke 19:11-27).
- Jesus Himself reported back to the One who sent Him (John 17:6-18).

Accountability is important not simply because it is modeled in the Scriptures, but because accountability helps Christ's followers to give their utmost and perform their best.

The April 2007 issue of Evangelical Missions Quarterly published the conclusions of a survey of 450 "tent-making" mission workers, and came to the following conclusion:

> Workers who have a clear strategy for planting a church are very effective, while workers who do not have a clear church-planting strategy are normally ineffective. Laborers who have someone holding them accountable in ministry at least once a month have a better probability of being effective than those who are held accountable less frequently.[*]

A Case Study

My experience at the Bible League gave me many case studies from all over the world that illustrate the strategic value of numerical accountability. For example, Bible League's "Project Philip" Scripture placement programs include a training element in which ordinary church members, called "Philips" after the New Testament example in Acts 8, are taught simple skills that enable them to lead Bible studies with interested seekers. The objective is for the "Philip" to walk one or more seekers through a complete introductory Bible course, and eventually to baptism in a local church. The workers in each country count the Philips trained, the number of people who complete a discipleship course, and the number baptized. The following results were registered for a recent year of ministry:

---

[*] EMQ 43:2; April 2007, p. 174.

Results:	Armenia	Kazakhstan	Philippines
Philips Trained	1,596	90	11,965
Bible Study Grads	1,200	2,012	478,454
New Members	322	6	64,851

Note that Armenia reported 1,596 Philips trained and recorded 1,200 Bible study participants who completed the course of study, 322 of whom were discipled to the point of baptism in a local church. Contrast this with Kazakhstan, which reported 90 Philips trained, 2,012 graduates, and 6 baptisms; and with the Philippines that reported 11,965 Philips trained, 478,454 graduates, and 64,851 baptized. Why did Armenia train so many Philips but record so few graduates? Why did Kazakhstan record more graduates but so few baptisms? How could the Philippines record so many graduates and so many baptisms relative to the Philips trained?

Investigation revealed that one issue in Armenia is in the "seminars" where people are trained as Philips. Bible League discovered that the "seminar training mentality" is not conducive to ministry results, since seminar participants rarely do anything more than "attend" and "learn." In Armenia, the vast majority of the seminar attendees never sought to reach anyone with the Scriptures, accounting for the low ratio of those trained to those completing a course.

Kazakhstan had experienced a similar problem,

and dealt with the problem by reporting only those seminar attendees who actually led Bible studies with at least one potential disciple. The number trained in the seminars during 2003 was actually 1,400 people, but only 90 of these put their training into practice. Contrast the Philippines where there are no open training seminars. Weekly training takes place in small groups consisting of volunteers who have already demonstrated their commitment to witnessing activity. Philippines' ratios are further boosted by the continuing year-to-year activity of Philips who were trained in years past and continue to teach Project Philip courses to non-church members.

The leadership challenge in Kazakhstan and Armenia is to limit training only to those true "Philips" who act on the Holy Spirit's call to seek out Ethiopians, or perhaps to improve the training experience so that it motivates more of the recipients to get to work. Kazakhstan training is now by individual invitation only, and applicants are interviewed in advance to ascertain their commitment to ministry.

Ministries are immeasurably strengthened when workers are accountable for results. As illustrated in the above example, such accountability requires the discipline of counting. The root of the word "accountability" is the word "count."

Biblical Priority

In the parables of the Sower (Matt. 13; Mark 4; Luke 8),

the Pounds (Luke 19), and the Talents (Matt. 25), counting the fruit of stewardship activity is central to each message. Without the numbers, the parables would not make sense. Nor could God's judgment on the unproductive stewards be understood.

In the three parables of the Lost in Luke 15, arranged according to descending ratios of the lost (one out of a hundred sheep, one out of ten coins, and one out of two sons), Jesus stresses the accountability of shepherds, housewives, and younger sons, and calls the Pharisees to account for their lack of compassion for the lost souls that God seeks to restore.

In Acts 27:37-44, not a single one of the 276 shipwrecked passengers was lost, a measure of God's accountability for the promises given by the angelic messenger to Paul (Acts 27:23-24). The individuals were important enough to God, to Paul, and to Luke that they counted every one of them that was saved from death.

We count those things that are important to us. *The World Christian Encyclopedia* reports, "Christians spend more on the annual audits of their churches and agencies ($810 million) than on all their workers in the non-Christian world." [†] Virtually every single Christian agency counts their money coming in and their money going out, and anyone who failed to do so would not long survive. But what else do we count?

---

† Barrett and Johnson, World Christian Trends, p. 3.

It's an axiom of management that you measure what is important to you. There is also a related truth: What you are asked to measure *becomes* important to you. Measuring systems strongly affect people's behavior. So it follows that when we measure what God accomplishes, we will be much more likely to praise Him for what He has done.

Biblical accountability has a significant spiritual dimension. When we report what God has accomplished, we are obeying the second most frequently repeated command in the Bible. Second only to the love commandments is the command to "Report what God has done."

We usually translate that as "Praise God" or "Glorify God." A way to praise, glorify, or honor God is to recount the good and powerful things that He has done. Virtually every psalm of praise illustrates the connection between praising God and reporting what He has done. For instance, the definition of praise is given in Psalm 106:2: "Who can proclaim the mighty acts of the Lord / Or fully declare his praise?"

In this case the synonymous parallelism of the Hebrew poetry makes it clear that to "proclaim the mighty acts of the Lord" is equivalent to "fully declare his praise." The same definition is seen in the parallelism of Psalm 105:2: "Sing to him, sing praise to him; / Tell of all his wonderful acts."

The psalms are full of examples. Psalm 66 for instance

alternates between exhortations to praise God and descriptions of God's saving activity:

> Shout with joy to God, all the earth!
> Sing the glory of his name;
> Make His praise glorious!
> Say to God, "How awesome are your deeds!
> So great is your power that your enemies cringe
> before you...
> Come and see what God has done,
> How awesome his works in man's behalf!
> He turned the sea into dry land,
> They passed through the waters on foot—
> Come, let us rejoice in him...
> Come and listen all you who fear God;
> Let me tell you what he has done for me...
> Praise be to God,
> Who has not rejected my prayer
> Or withheld his love from me!

Virtually all 72 verses of Psalm 78 are narrative reports of what the Psalm itself calls God's "praiseworthy deeds" (Ps. 78:4). Psalm 96 also defines "praise" when the psalmist exhorts us: "Declare his glory among the nations, his marvelous deeds among all peoples. For great is the Lord and most worthy of praise" (Ps. 96:3-4). Psalm 103 does the same: "Praise the Lord, O my soul, and forget not all his benefits—who forgives all your sins and heals all your diseases" (Ps. 103:2-3).

This connection between praise and reporting what someone has done is assumed in our ordinary use of the word *praise*. When my son's or daughter's school teacher praises either, the teacher will be basing that on what my child said or did. When a business executive praises his employees, he tells them or others what activities or accomplishments merit his praise.

Reporting what God has done is very important to God. This activity forms the core of our witness in calling people to trust Jesus—we report to them what God has already accomplished for them in Christ. This is the Good News. After people become disciples, this activity continues to engage us as we, like the authors of the Scriptures, tell others what God has performed in our lives and in the lives of converts.

- When I report back to someone who has been praying for my ministry, describing how God has performed a miracle of transformation in an individual or family, I am praising and glorifying God.

- When I report back to those who have been praying and giving in order to reach the lost, when I list the numbers of people and places where God's Word has triumphed, I am praising and glorifying God.

- When I report back to someone who has given

me money to do God's work, detailing the various expenses that were covered by their gift, I am praising God for His provision for the work to which He has called me.

- When I ask a ministry partner for her report back to me, giving me the details of lives changed, communities reached, or funds expended, I am asking her to praise and glorify God. I am not asking any more than God Himself asks and desires of each one of us.

Focusing on what God has accomplished is essential to measuring what matters. In genuine humility, we acknowledge that spiritual accomplishments always belong to God, not to any human agency or person. When other servants of Christ also report what God has accomplished through their ministries, we rejoice with them, not as competitors but as fellow servants of Christ.

The Greater Spiritual Returns

The spiritual dynamic in an accountability relationship results not only in bringing glory to God, it also results in greater spiritual returns. Asking people to praise God by reporting on specific things that God has accomplished through them serves to focus everyone on the most important ministry activities.

The head of a large mission agency that serves as a Mission India partner in India gave a testimony that is typical of Mission India reporting partners:

> When you first asked us for written reports, we were very reluctant. Reporting is difficult for us. We did not like to do it. It takes a lot of time and effort. We wanted to account only to God. But now that we have been reporting back to you over the past two years, I cannot believe our great results. These reports have helped us to focus our efforts. We have never had such success in our ministries. We never believed that we could accomplish so much for God. We now require such reporting from all our workers.

The largest Mission India program with the most reporting partners is the Children's Bible Club (CBC) ministry. A few years back, during a period of heightened persecution against Christians, Mission India staff stopped requesting CBC partners to report how many people were baptized as a consequence of the Bible Clubs. This was because persecution most often results when people are baptized, so Mission India staff feared that the request for baptismal information was itself endangering some partners. Other reports were still required, just not the number of baptisms.

A couple of years later, the request for baptism information resumed. Partners in one region where persecution is prevalent began to report hundreds more baptisms than had ever before been experienced. Many of them told stories similar to one leader's confession:

> When you began asking us again how many
> people were baptized, we realized that we were not
> doing our work properly. We were not preparing
> converts for baptism. Your request reminded us
> of God's command. So now, whenever we see
> your question "how many people received water
> baptism?" our workers are encouraged to remind
> the new believers, "You must be baptized." As a
> result the churches are greatly strengthened.

It's a well-known business principle: whatever you ask your staff to measure and report, that is most likely where they will invest and focus their greatest efforts. If you are only reporting dollars raised and dollars spent, then inevitably your staff will focus their efforts on the money, rather than the ministry. If you are reporting Bibles printed, then the focus will be on the printing of paper-and-ink products, rather than whether anyone is reading or benefiting from them. If you are a crusade evangelist and you are reporting "people who came forward to the stage to receive Christ," then the focus will be on what happens during the night of the crusade, whether or not any new members were added to local churches.

If you are reporting how many new churches were established, then the process of planting new worshipping congregations will receive your energy and efforts. Whatever you decide to measure and report, that is where you eventually will invest and focus your greatest efforts.

Accountability in Teams

Tiya Putot was a very poor, middle-aged woman who along with her husband had been led to Christ by a gifted evangelist working among poor farm workers in rural Negros Island in the Philippines. She and her husband lived in a one-room, thatch-roofed shack, and sometimes there was not enough food for their children. One of the first benefits of their conversion was that her husband had stopped wasting money on liquor, leaving more for their family's daily necessities.

I was meeting with the elders of their church, and Tiya Putot was the topic of discussion. A deacon had observed Tiya Putot at the house of a neighbor, sitting around a table under the mango tree with three other women. The loud clacking of Mahjong tiles echoed through the little neighborhood as the women played their game. They were having a great time. Problem was, Mahjong is a notoriously addictive gambling game, and Tiya Putot was arguably throwing away her family's precious resources as she played. The pastor had preached often about the dangers of gambling, and in the case of the poorest of the poor, dangers that could result in the deaths of malnourished children.

Two elders were assigned to go to Tiya Putot with a severe reprimand. For several weeks afterward, neither Tiya nor her husband was seen in any of the church's worship services or meetings.

After a few weeks, I happened to see Tiya's husband one day while passing through the town, and I stopped to talk to him. I told him how sorry I was that he was not in church recently. He said, "Sir, I'm ashamed to come because we are being disciplined for my wife's gambling."

I said to him, "But it's only Tiya who is being disciplined. You are not being disciplined, so you can come to the service."

To which he replied, "How can you say this? Don't you know that my wife and I use the same toothbrush?"

Eventually Tiya and her husband were restored to fellowship, and Tiya gave up her gambling. And along the way, they taught me the importance of the team. As far as their public life was concerned, without a second thought, Tiya and her husband considered themselves to be a close-knit team, and therefore to be intimately responsible for each other's actions. Team members will not always use the same toothbrush, but all true teams share experiences that are unique to their group. The closeness of team members leads to a spiritual dynamic of mutual accountability.

One of the reasons that Jesus sent out workers two by two, and an important reason why many agencies train workers in teams, is that healthy teams always include a natural accountability factor. Team members who come together repeatedly in small group classrooms to learn together, pray together, share experiences, and listen to one another, are effectively using the same toothbrush. They always perform better than individuals who work alone. Team members naturally care what their co-workers think, and naturally account to one another for their activities. It just happens. It's a work that the Holy Spirit does in the hearts of people bound together by their common task. It's a work of encouragement.

"Lone rangers" are less productive and less successful than workers who labor as part of a larger team. This is not only because lone rangers lack the diverse gifts that teams bring to a task, but also because lone rangers lack the accountability structures that are always inherent in teams. Team members communicate with one another, even when reporting is not structured into their relationship. This natural "fellowship" of communicated events serves as an informal spiritual accountability relationship, and greatly reinforces and motivates the participants in the activities or objectives that they share in common.

The team usually includes those who give money and offer prayers for our success. Accountability in reporting is the action that affirms our reliance on all the team members that the Lord has blessed us with.

{ 11

The Limits of Measuring

We've looked at many examples of how missions organizations can benefit from measuring their progress in accomplishing the Great Commission. But there's no question that drawbacks exist to keeping count, especially in a world marked by suspicion, conflicting motives, and political manipulation.

Measuring Is Not Easy

Population data in some countries is so controversial and politicized that objectivity seems impossible. What percent of Nigerians are nominally Muslim? What percent of India is nominally Hindu? How many Christians worship in unregistered churches in China? Answers vary. Reports cannot be entirely trusted because political agendas inhibit the numbering process in these and other countries.

Fuzzy Numbers

Mark Twain's aphorism, "figures don't lie, but liars figure," came out of his experience with evil manipulators of statistics. Christians are not exempt. David Barrett claims, "Some 250 of the 300 largest international Christian organizations regularly mislead the Christian public by publishing demonstrably incorrect or falsified progress statistics" and that "Christian triumphalism—not as pride in huge numbers, but as publicized self-congratulation—is rampant in most churches, agencies, and ministries." * Undoubtedly such attitudes contribute to suspicion regarding numerical reports.

False Motives

The often-cited instance of King David's numbering of the people of Israel illustrates the sin of numbering for evil purposes (2 Sam. 24). The problem, however, was obviously not the act of counting. By contrast, God provided extremely detailed instructions for numbering the people of Israel who were marching as God's army through the wilderness, thus the name of that portion of the Pentateuch that we know as *"The Book of Numbers."* This numbering happened not once, but twice during the forty years in the wilderness (Num. 2:32-34; 26:51, 63-65). It illustrates the fact that numbering does not devalue but actually enhances the value of what is being counted. It's not the numbering that is bad, but the abuse of numbering that limits our use of measurements. Our numbers should be accurate, and should always direct our primary attention and loyalty to God Himself.

---

* Barrett and Johnson, *World Christian Trends*, p. 3.

Reality Check

Measuring has limited value when statistics become disconnected from the reality they are describing. When this happens numbering can have a numbing effect. No one can imagine in his mind's eye the reality of 10,000 individual human beings, much less a million or a billion. So it is tempting to let our minds focus fuzzily on "10,000 *people*" rather than focus concretely on "10,000 living, breathing *individual human beings.*"

It Is Always Personal

Do numbers inherently depersonalize people, robbing them of their personal worth? Not necessarily. No one can imagine 10,000 human hairs, and yet Jesus promises that "even the very hairs of your head are all numbered," an indication of the high value that God places on every individual believer (Matt. 10:30). When measuring what matters, it is important to tell the personal stories that illustrate that it is not the numbers themselves, but their referents that are important to us.

Conclusion

There is one other limit to numbering, a limitation that every disciple of Jesus longs to experience. The prophet Hosea foresaw the day when the people of God would be too numerous to be counted (Hos. 1:10). John the Seer had the same vision: He saw "ten thousand times ten thousand" (Rev. 5:11) and "a great multitude that no one could count" (Rev. 7:9). Surely the vision of this un-countable multitude does not depersonalize or de-value the individual human souls whose robes, we are told in the same chapter, were washed in the blood of the Lamb (Rev. 7:14) and who will have God Himself "wipe away every tear from their eyes" (Rev. 7:17).

I think often about the great multitude around the throne of God, waving banners of victory and singing the praises of their Lord and Savior. I wonder whom I will be standing next to. I wonder what we will talk about. I am convinced that we will not only sing, "Salvation belongs to our God, who sits on the throne, and to the Lamb" (Rev. 7:10). We will also get specific. We will tell each other our own stories of salvation that give flesh and blood to what God has accomplished. He has accomplished a lot, so thankfully we will have an eternity to recount His results. It will be "accountability made perfect."

In the meantime, let us measure what matters as best we can.

Appendix

Three Key Great Commission Measures

Every ministry can measure its progress. Some will count how many poor people have been fed. Others will count how many children adopted, how many languages translated, how many pastors trained, how many viewers watched the film, how many addicts counseled, or how many students graduated. What you count becomes part of your bottom line and the reason to ask others to invest their time, talent, and treasures in your ministry.

Not all ministries are Great Commission ministries. For those who claim to be, the Great Commission and related texts prioritize at least three measurable ministry outcomes:

1. individual disciples made,

2. disciples gathered into new local churches, and

3. people groups (Greek *ethne*) in which disciples are made or churches established.

The Great Commission will become the Great Completion when every people group counts among its members those whom God has called to be disciples of Jesus, meeting together as the gathered church of Jesus, ready to join their brothers and sisters around the Great Throne in heaven.

The task of establishing churches of disciples among every people group is not yet finished:

1. Worldwide, there are approximately 7 billion people, of whom 2 billion have never heard the name of Jesus; and another 2.6 billion have received the Gospel in some form but have not responded by becoming disciples.[*]

2. Worldwide, there are approximately 7 million human communities (villages, neighborhoods, barrios, etc…), of which 2 million have no identifiable church in their midst.

3. Worldwide, there are approximately 16,000 "people groups" (ethne), of which 6,000 are not yet reached with a viable church population of Jesus' disciples in their midst.[†]

Any individual or organization that aims to make a measurable impact on the unfinished task should be able to track and report regarding three objectives:

---

[*] "Status of Global Mission 2011," Center for the Study of Global Christianity, accessed January 27, 2011.
http://www.gordonconwell.edu/resources/documents/StatusOfGlobalMission.pdf

[†] See for instance, Justin Long, "Least Reached Peoples," Mission Frontiers, May-June 2006, page 9.

1. How many individuals became disciples?

2. How many new churches were established?

3. How many unreached people groups were populated with new churches and new disciples?

Each of these three measures needs definition. What observable behavior determines whether a person has become a disciple? How do you define a church? What determines whether a people group is reached or not yet reached?

To a great extent, even the definitions of these categories will require measuring activity. For instance, the largest Protestant denominations in Romania define a local "church" as one that has at least 30 adult members on its rolls. An unreached people group is defined as one that has no indigenous church that has sufficient resources to theoretically evangelize its own people without major cross-cultural missionary assistance. For the sake of definition, this includes those groups that are less than 2% evangelical Christian and less than 5% Christian adherents.[‡]

Using consistent definitions from year to year, a Great Commission ministry can keep track of its progress by tallying year-by-year these three measures of Great Commission impact.

[‡] For an explanation of these numbers see: www.joshuaproject.net/definitions.php#unreached.